MW00379965

INSITE 2011
PERSHING'S FINANCIAL SOLUTIONS CONFERENCE

Tres Arnett

George W. (Tres) Arnett III

Morgan Lewis   **Pershing**
                      A BNY MELLON COMPANY

Additional Praise for
Global Securities Markets

"In der Beschränkung zeigt sich erst der Meister (Goethe) and that's what it is. All this historic explanatory and practical information within less than 200 pages. My compliments!! That makes it a "must have" for experienced professionals as well as ambitious newcomers to the industry."
—**Bert Van Delft, Directeur Operations, Binck Bank, Amsterdam**

"Mr. Arnett has created that rare publication that is versatile enough to educate the securities professional, the practicing attorney, and the member of the investing public and entertaining enough for all three."
—**David Campbell, General Counsel,
Silvercrest Asset Management, New York**

"A book that should be on every securities professional's desk"
—**Matt Rochlin, Vice Chairman,
The Williams Capital Group, New York**

"A well-researched and informative work, covering a broad spectrum of issues and topics pertinent to the global securities markets—a must-read for securities professionals and global investors."
—**Karen Tiah, Partner, Allen & Gledhill LLP, Singapore**

"Tres Arnett has made it easy to understand all the things we had to figure out for ourselves, and then automate and improve."
—**Gates Hawn, former Global Head of Financial Services,
Credit Suisse, New York**

Global
Securities
Markets

Global Securities Markets

Navigating the World's Exchanges and OTC Markets

GEORGE W. ARNETT III

John Wiley & Sons, Inc.

Published by John Wiley & Sons, Inc., Hoboken, New Jersey.
Published simultaneously in Canada.

For general information on our other products and services or for technical support, please
contact our Customer Care Department within the United States at (800) 762–2974, outside
the United States at (317) 572–3993 or fax (317) 572–4002.

Wiley also publishes its books in a variety of electronic formats. Some content that appears in
print may not be available in electronic books. For more information about Wiley products,
visit our web site at www.wiley.com.

Library of Congress Cataloging-in-Publication Data:

Arnett, George W., III
   Global Securities Markets: Navigating the World's Exchanges and OTC Markets /
George W. Arnett, III.
      p. cm. – (Wiley Finance ; 670)
   Includes bibliographical references and index.
ISBN 978-1-118-02771-4 (hardback); 978-1-118-05660-8 (ebk);
978-1-118-05661-5 (ebk); 978-1-118-05662-2 (ebk)
   1. Stock exchanges–Case studies.   2. Over-the-counter markets–Case studies.
3. Investments–Case studies.   I. Title.
   HG4551.A734 2011
   332.64′2–dc22

                                                                    2010050387

Printed in the United States of America

10 9 8 7 6 5 4 3 2 1

To my father and grandfather, both of whom were stockbrokers and my first guides to the securities markets; and to my entire family.

Contents

Foreword

The financial markets touch all of our lives. If you didn't believe that in years past, you surely do now after the tumultuous events of the late 2000s.

The workings and integrity of those markets are vital to our increasingly global and interconnected economies.

If you've chosen a career that involves working in the securities industry, you have a front-row seat in a dynamic and sometimes unpredictable field. George (Tres) Arnett and I met many years ago at Yale University where we both studied economics. And we have both spent our careers connected to the financial services industry. The Tres I remember from those days was intelligent, articulate, interesting, purposeful, and ethical. This book is a reflection of those values and attributes.

Tres's new book can help you to learn the rich history of the global securities markets, how those markets work, and important legal concepts. In short, Tres's book will make you more competent in your field and better informed. And, it should make you a better investor!

ERIC TYSON
Syndicated Columnist
Best-Selling Author, Investing for Dummies *and*
    Personal Finance for Dummies *(John Wiley & Sons)*
www.erictyson.com
February 1, 2011

Preface

This book is Global Securities Markets 101. But it is not a dry textbook. It is full of rich history, interesting anecdotes, and understandable mathematical and legal concepts. There is no book quite like it anywhere that weaves together all the facets of the global securities market and tells the tale in plain readable English, at a high global level, and in less than 200 entertaining pages. And it is a feature of this book, like the hub of a wheel arrayed with spokes, to point the reader to the right materials by Internet link or further reading sources for more information on any given topic.

The lodestar for this guidebook is the familiar five-point star known as a pentagram. For many (Christians, Jews, and Taoists, to name a few), the pentagram is a symbol of faith. For ancient Greeks, the pentagram represented mathematical perfection. And for some, a pentagram contains dark forces and magic. In many ways, the global securities market embodies everything in the symbology associated with a pentagram star. Markets exist on the faith that one party will exchange with another. Markets thrive on mathematical precision. And markets can be mysterious.

However, the global securities market is not sorcery. Using the pentagram illustration featured in Chapter 1, concise explanations, and other graphic presentations, this book seeks to demystify the global securities markets for market participants as well as the educated investor.

There is an emphasis on history, because, as Oliver Wendell Holmes Jr. famously declared, "A page of history is worth a volume of logic." There is also an emphasis on graphic presentation so the reader can easily visualize complex material.

I would like to thank a number of my Pershing and Bank of New York Mellon colleagues as well as our customers who have provided valuable suggestions and input in connection with the creation of this book. Ethan Johnson Esq. of Morgan, Lewis & Bockius (www.morganlewis.com) and Ajay Pathak Esq., as well as Alex Leitch, Esq., of SJ Berwin (www.sjberwin.com) provided additional legal expertise. Charlie Saulenas created the graphics. Ana Pierro, Daiana Urena, Chenice Brinson, Jodi Vitale, Olga Pavez, and

Mary Neufeld organized it all. Last, I would like to thank my wife, M'lou, for her support during the creation of this book, as well as my children (who inspired the idea for the star pentagram chart).

GEORGE W. (TRES) ARNETT III
Jersey City
February 2011

Introduction

With more than 190 countries in the world, 320 distinct legal jurisdictions, 110 securities exchanges, 40 derivatives exchanges, and a withering notional value of over-the-counter derivatives and alternative investments regularly bought and sold, investing in the global securities markets poses challenges beyond selecting a suitable security likely to provide a decent return on investment.

In the sections that follow, we touch on fundamental concepts such as the definition of a security; the mechanics of execution, clearing, settlement, and custody; and the development and regulation of exchange markets and market participants. For those interested in global equity investing, we set forth the principal exchanges around the world and their most actively traded stocks with Internet links for more information. In addition to covering margin, short selling, and prime brokerage, we also examine briefly the evolving disciplines of risk management, anti-money laundering, and international compliance. For the high-net-worth investor, there is a short chapter on managed accounts. In brief, it is the theme of this book to tie everything together for the global investor (and those who support him) so that a clear and broad picture emerges of the legal, commercial, and practical aspects of the global securities markets.

Since the law, regulation and practice developed in the United States, United Kingdom, and European markets inform the worldwide marketplace for securities, our vantage point is principally United States, United Kingdom, and European law and practice. Distinctions among these markets and others around the world are noted.

CHAPTER 1

Fundamental Concepts

Figure 1.1 encapsulates the typical flow of the global securities market and serves as a framework for review. Although this chapter is elementary in approach, the educated professional should enjoy the chapter because it provides rich context and a solid foundation for the material that follows.

At the bottom of the chart (the Earth if you will) are the issuers of securities—corporations, sovereigns, and all of the many legal entities that comprise the debt and equity market worldwide.

The investor is at the bottom-left-hand corner of the great pentagram in the chart. The investor decides to buy a security using a broker. The broker needs to locate a security so the broker seeks out a place where there is a market—an exchange. The exchange provides liquidity—an active, readily available market in those securities. The exchange members are linked to a clearing system whereby the seller of the security (via a broker) ratifies an order with the buyer (via the buyer's broker). The clearing system is linked to a central securities depository through which the two market participants deliver securities and settle payment. At the central custodian, the investor's securities are held in safekeeping through the intermediation of a broker or bank. And as neatly and as quickly as one could draw a star, the securities pentagram is made manifest.

Overlooking the securities universe, like the sun, are the regulators. Like the moon driving the inexorable tides, the transfer agent reconciles—day in and day out—the securities' positions among the depositories and the issuers of securities.

With this overview graphically embedded in our minds, we examine the features of the global securities firmament in greater detail.

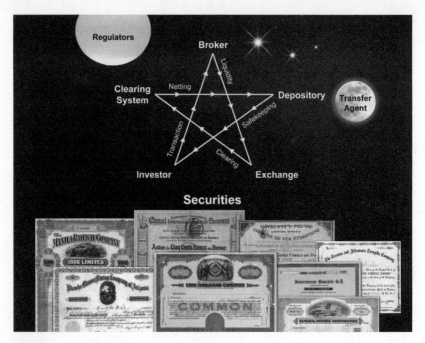

FIGURE 1.1 The Global Markets Pentagram

LEGAL DEFINITION OF SECURITY

A security, unlike goods or land, has no utilitarian value. A security is simply a manifestation of a promise by an issuer to pay interest and return capital in the case of bonds, or share in the ownership of a company in the case of stock. In truth, a security is hard to define. It is not a check; but it can be a note.[1] In many cases, the law resorts to a list in order to define what a security actually is.

---

[1]*Reves v. Ernst & Young*, 494 U.S. 56 (1990). What is and is not a security has meaning, particularly in the United States, because the definition may dictate what body (for example, the Commodity Futures Trading Commissions [CFTC] or the Securities and Exchange Commission [SEC]) regulates the activity in the financial instrument. For example, only some derivatives, notably options, are deemed to be "securities" in the United States. As a matter of statutory definition in the United States, other derivatives (such as interest rate swaps and credit default swaps) escaped traditional securities regulation because they were largely thought to be purchased by sophisticated investors. The failure to regulate derivatives is thought by many to be one of the causes of the 2008–2009 recession (see Chapter 10). Although interests in investment partnerships are most often considered securities, the offering of these investment instruments also follows a regulatory path designed for sophisticated investors.

Bonds

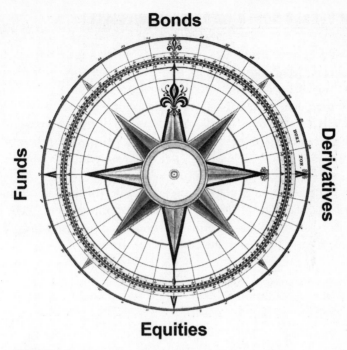

Funds

Derivatives

Equities

FIGURE 1.2 The Securities Compass

Conceptually, a security can be defined as an investment pooled with others and managed by third parties with whom the investors participate in the economic fate of a common enterprise (whether it be a sovereign nation or a corporation). Securities include equities, options on securities, warrants, preferred shares, depository receipts, bonds, debentures, collateralized debt and mortgage obligations, and mutual funds. A hallmark feature of a security is transferability in a readily available market. In order to further orient ourselves, a comparison to a compass may prove helpful as shown in Figure 1.2.

Imagine the four points of a compass. North are bonds and South are equities. East are derivatives (such as listed options or credit default swaps) and West are investment funds. Anywhere on the compass, depending on the characteristics of the security, one can array a financial investment because they all tend toward one coordinate or another. Although the precise feature of every security is beyond the scope of this book, we will examine the principal coordinates on the compass.

NORTH VERSUS SOUTH (DEBT VERSUS EQUITY)

Issuers of debt securities induce suppliers of capital (*rentiers*[2] in the language of the French economist) to part with their money in the exchange for the promise of payment of a complete return of capital plus interest[3] at some future point in time. This is the essence of a debt security.[4] Although colloquially referred to as bonds, there is a legal difference between a bond (which guarantees payment of the debt with a pledge of property) and a debenture (another French word), which has only a corporation's future profits as security for future payment.

With the adoption of the law merchant into the English common law by Lord Mansfield in the 1700s, a vibrant and international debt market emerged.[5] Currently, the debt market (including government and quasi-government debt, but not including loans by banks) is approximately

---

[2]The French via a group of economic writers known as the *Physiocrats* gave us many of the words of modern finance. Arguably the first school of political economic thought, the Physiocrats placed an emphasis on protecting and developing a nation's agriculture. Later, Adam Smith, in *The Wealth of Nations*, articulated the benefits of manufacturing and free trade. It is interesting to note, however, the protectionist doctrine of the Physiocrats (and their predecessors, the Mercantilists) still manifests itself in national policy (such as exchange controls, discussed in Chapter 13).

[3]"I do not know what the seven wonders of the world are, but I do know the eighth: compound interest," said Baron Rothschild (1840–1915). Compound interest is easily described as adding interest to interest at some agreed periodic time frame. For a detailed explanation of future value, present value and yield calculation as well as an in-depth explanation of various fixed income securities and bond portfolio management, one can review Frank J. Fabozzi, *The Handbook of Fixed Income Securities* 5th ed. (Irwin Professional 1996).

[4]The Islamic world views charging interest as morally reprehensible. Many Christians (St. Augustine being a notable example) have taken the same view (although usually limited to not charging extortionate rates). *Exodus* 22:25–27. All people must evolve legal structures in order to advance, so Muslims developed the "Sukuk," which is akin to a repurchase agreement in which a putative borrower sells an item in return for cash and then the borrower agrees to buy it back at some future time, only at higher price, thereby effectively paying the lender for the use of the money. A similar practice emerged among money changers in Lombard, Italy after a papal decree prohibited interest-bearing loans between Christians. In time, "Lombards," as these new money changers came to be known, developed collateralized loan techniques that spread throughout Europe. A vocation among Jews and, later, Quakers, a nascent banking diaspora spread throughout Europe and then to the United States. Even today, many major European cities have a Lombard Street and some still refer to collateralized loans as "Lombard loans." Quakers and Jews were not the only religious groups with an impact on the markets. For an interesting perspective on the Puritans' impact on business and finance from the 1630s to the present day refer to, Kenneth and William Hopper, *The Puritan Gift* (I. B. Tauris 2007).

[5]See C.H.S. Fifoot, *Lord Mansfield* (Oxford University Press 1899). The "law merchant" refers to the customs developed among merchants concerning their dealings in goods and negotiable instruments. Justice Joseph Story, in promoting legal precepts that aided the development of

$91 trillion. Compare this figure to the equity market of $52 trillion (market value of issued shares) and one can see why the efficient trading of debt has been a principal focus of efficient trading, clearance, settlement, and custody. In fact, the two largest international central securities depositories, Euroclear in Belgium and Clearstream in Luxembourg, were first developed as custodians of debt securities.

Interest, of course, is the amount of money paid to the rentier for the use of his capital, usually expressed as a percentage, calculated in a variety of ways, but spelled out in a contractual document binding on the borrower. The document is an indenture. The corporate trust department of a bank typically acts as indenture trustee, collecting the issuer's bond interest payments and paying them to the bondholders in accordance with the indenture's terms. Under this scenario, the debt holder is a secured creditor of the debt issuer. In contrast, the equity owner (or ordinary shareholder, as the English would say) holds a claim to corporate assets subordinated to the bondholder and relegated to a residual claim on corporate property.

EAST VERSUS WEST (DERIVATIVES VERSUS FUNDS)

Investment funds come in various forms—mutual funds (open-end companies investing in liquid securities), exchange-traded funds (ETFs), closed-end funds (listed funds that are similar to ETFs), hedge funds, private equity funds, venture capital funds, and real estate funds. The primary features of all of these investment funds are the diversification of risk, limitation of liability, and third-party management. Investment funds can be organized in many ways and in many different countries. The form of organization is often determined by the nature of the investments. For example, U.S. mutual funds are typically organized as Delaware, Maryland, or Massachusetts corporations or business trusts permitting daily redemptions and subscriptions and are transparent (by election with the IRS) for tax purposes—meaning that income, gains, and losses are deemed to be received by the investor rather than the fund. The European equivalent of the U.S. mutual fund, UCITs, are organized along similar lines. On the other hand, private equity

---

commerce, did the same thing for the United States that Lord Mansfield had done for England. See, e.g., *Charles River Bridge v. Warren Bridge*, 36. U.S. 420 (1837). By the 1830s the London market was awash with U.S. corporate debt (canals, railroads, turnpikes, and other enterprises), which competed with sovereign debt for the rentier's capital. "The barometer of the American money market hangs up at the Stock Exchange in London," said one congressman in 1833. See Ron Chernow, *The House of Morgan* (Simon & Schuster 1991).

funds and hedge funds, which typically invest in less liquid securities and are not offered to the public, are typically structured as Delaware limited partnerships (or LLCs) or companies with limited liability in the Cayman Islands, Luxembourg, or Ireland. This structure also provides for a tax transparency (in the case of partnerships) or tax exemption (in the case of funds organized in tax havens). Venture capital funds and real estate funds are structured along similar lines because they are also typically privately offered, do not have a need to provide short-term liquidity and benefit from the flexible capital account allocation opportunities available in the limited partnership structure. Many hedge funds are formed in offshore jurisdictions in order to exploit available tax exemptions; however, they generally do not want to be tax transparent for European and U.S. income tax purposes. This is important for non-U.S. investors in hedge funds with U.S. equity investments, as it provides a shield against U.S. estate taxes (inheritance taxes) and trade or business taxes. The structure is also useful for shielding U.S. tax-exempt investors from taxable income—specifically, unrelated business taxable income—that is generated by the fund using margin loans to purchase securities (rendering a portion of income derived from securities purchased with leverage subject to tax).

Given their popularity with retail investors, it is useful to spend a few moments on mutual funds. Mutual funds are in essence a claim to the portion of an investment fund based on the fund's net asset value. Particularly attractive to an investor seeking diversification because mutual funds typically invest across an array of securities, the amount of money in mutual funds has grown tremendously since they came on the scene in Massachusetts in the 1920s. However, the growth was relatively small from the 1930s through the 1970s, in part due to a loss of investor confidence in mutual funds after the collapse in the 1960s of a high-profile fund called International Overseas Services. In the mid-1990s in the United States, the average annual growth rate was 22.4 percent. Similarly, in Europe the average annual growth rate in the same time period was 17.7 percent. This growth, in part, stems from their inclusion as investment vehicles for defined contribution systems in the United States, Australia, New Zealand, and South Africa, among others. Hong Kong, Ireland, Singapore, Switzerland, and Luxembourg have a large number of nonresident mutual fund investors, in part, attracted to the low tax regime in those countries. Mutual fund investments stand in contrast to derivative securities whose values are derived from the value of another security based on a contract without a claim, however, to any underlying collective investment fund assets. Derivatives, conceptually, are much closer to bilateral contracts. Derivatives are discussed in greater detail in Chapter 10.

INVESTORS

Investors can be divided into two groups: retail investors and institutional investors. Retail investors—individuals investing in stocks for speculation or investments—are but a small fraction of the marketplace. Institutional investors—banks, insurance companies, pension funds, hedge funds, mutual fund companies—are by far the lion's share of the market. Particularly in Europe, but also around the world, the tendency is for law and regulation to protect the uninitiated but let the sophisticated investor fend for himself. For example, the British Virgin Islands allows an international business corporation to contract as it pleases with little regulation under the theory that it is a sophisticated corporate structure. In Germany, some courts treat derivatives investors with sophisticated prior investment experience differently than retail investors with no experience, mandating extensive disclosure to the latter and affording monetary relief to the unsophisticated investor if that disclosure was not made.

The scope of freedom of contract afforded to an investor also turns on whether the investor was solicited by a broker or whether the investor took the initiative and reached out to the broker. If the latter—and if the brokerage firm where the broker works has no physical presence in a country—then both investor and broker may escape financial regulation. In Chile, for example, where there is no public offer of securities in country, Chilean investors are free to contract with whomever they like and accept the application of laws governing their contracts that are outside of Chile. It is these dual-related concepts—solicitation and sophistication—on which the international regulation of dealings between brokers and their customers turns.[6]

BROKERS, BANKS, AND ADVISORS

Once known as a *customer's man*, a broker intermediates between his customer and the market. Typically, a broker is a licensed professional employed by an investment firm. The investment firm will provide him with an order management system, access to exchanges, and books and records

---

[6]Jurisdiction-by-jurisdiction analysis of solicitation of customers, conduct of business rules, and other cross-border legal and compliance issues can be found in Barnabas Reynolds, *International Financial Markets Guide* (Lexis Nexis Butterworths, 2003).

functionality (such as the issuance of confirmations of transactions to the broker's customers and the publication of periodic statements to the broker's customers of their holdings and transactions). In a classic investment firm model, the firm would provide investment banking[7] services for the issuers of securities and distribute those securities through the brokers. The investment firm would give the brokers research about the issue being distributed as well as research on other stocks from which the brokers could select suitable investments for their customers. Brokers are paid a commission on a per-transaction basis.

In some jurisdictions, brokers are distinguished from investment advisors. Investment advisors provide investment advice for a set fee. In the United States, advisors are held to a slightly higher standard of care with their customers than brokers. For example, where brokers must recommend suitable transactions and must not act unjustly or inequitably, advisors are held to a fiduciary standard, meaning they must always put the customers' interests ahead of their own.

Banks and bank officers (whether trust officers or private bankers) may recommend securities transactions as well, but (as a general rule) they employ brokers to execute those transactions. Banks play a much larger role in the securities industry as custodians for institutional investors or indenture trustees or as sponsors for depositary receipts.

PHYSICAL SECURITIES

When securities take a physical form, possession of a certificate in bearer form (or possession of the certificate with a lawful assignment) is the key to establishing successful legal ownership. A quick review in this chapter of fundamental concepts establishes the context for the more complicated issues of perfected liens and electronic ownership through securities intermediaries discussed in Chapter 7. Examine this Hungarian governmental obligation (shown in Figure 1.3).

---

[7]It is interesting to note that just as the rise of securitized mortgages has replaced the role of the savings banks, private equity firms have replaced the role of investment banks in marrying investment capital with firms that need capital. Gone are the days of "3-6-3" when the small-town savings banker paid depositors 3 percent, lent homeowners money at 6 percent, and was on the golf course by three o'clock. Gone, too, are the major investment banks, which are now banks themselves or are owned by banks.

FIGURE 1.3 Bearer Bond and Coupon

This bond, of course, represents a promise by the government of Hungary, backed by the government's ability to collect taxes, to pay the principal amount owed and the stated interest amount. In this case, the government's agent, a bank, pays the interest due upon presentation of a coupon that has been clipped from the bond and delivered to the bank for payment (a coupon is shown under the bond). Ownership is evidenced by possession of the bond and coupon.

AGENCY

An agent is someone with whom a principal contracts to perform a service for the principal at the principal's direction. An agent is frequently someone who can commit his principal (e.g., bind the principal to a contract). When you ask your broker to obtain 100 shares of Underwater Aircraft stock for you, the broker acts as your agent and you are the principal. An attorney-in-fact (as opposed to an attorney-at-law) is the principal's appointed agent. An example of the appointment of an attorney-in-fact is embedded in the stock power presented in Figure 1.4. A stock power is a physical piece of paper typically attached to the physical certificate used to legally transfer ownership of the certificate from one person to another. In the day of paper certificates, this power of assignment was required by the transfer agent to transfer all physical stock certificates after the original issuance by the corporation. When presented to the transfer agent, the records as to securities ownership of the company were changed, the old certificate was cancelled and a new one was issued, and the new owner became a registered holder with all the rights of ownership, including the right to vote and receive dividends (in the case of a stock) or to receive interest payments (in the case of bonds).

PURCHASE AND SALE OF SECURITIES AND THE DEVELOPMENT OF EXCHANGES

In the first instance, the purchase and sale of a security can be purely a private affair between two individuals. Theoretically, nothing legally stops

---

IRREVOCABLE STOCK OR BOND POWER

FOR VALUE RECEIVED, the undersigned does (do) hereby sell, assign and transfer to

_____

_____

_____

IF STOCK,
COMPLETE
THIS
PORTION

_____ shares of the _____ stock of _____

represented by Certificate(s) No(s). _____

inclusive, standing in the name of the undersigned on the books of said Company.

IF BONDS,
COMPLETE
THIS
PORTION

_____ bonds of _____

in principal amount of $ _____, No(s)_____

inclusive, standing in the name of the undersigned on the books of said Company

The undersigned does (do) hereby irrevocably constitute and appoint _____

_____attorney to transfer the said stock or bonds (s),

as the case may be, on the books of said Company, with full power of substitution

in the premises.

Dated _____

IMPORTANT - READ CAREFULLY
The signature(s) to this Power must correspond
with the name(s) as written upon the face of the
certificate(s) or bond(s) in every particular without alteration or enlargement or any change what-
ever. Signature guarantee should be made by a
member or member organization of the New York
Stock Exchange, members of other Exchanges
having signatures on file with transfer agent or by
a commercial bank or trust company having its
principal office or correspondent in the City of
New York.
C133- Irrevocable Stock or Bond Power

_____

_____

(PERSON(S) EXECUTING THIS POWER SIGN(S) HERE)
SIGNATURE IS GUARANTEED

FIGURE 1.4 Sample Stock Power

the private sale of the Hungarian bond in the earlier example or the private sale of stock accompanied by a valid stock power.[8]

Trading markets emerged when people gathered to trade stocks and bonds, and soon buyers and sellers started employing agents (brokers) to buy and sell stock for them. The brokers themselves banded together to buy and sell, moved their operations out of the coffeehouses and alleyways, and created the exchanges.[9] A principal feature of the new exchanges was that brokers would only trade with each other and they would charge specified fixed commissions.

Markets in shares really burst onto the world stage in the early eighteenth century. As European governments looked to new ways to finance the debt of wars and extravagant kings, they granted exclusive charters to companies to exploit the New World in exchange for the new companies assuming government debt. The new companies issued securities to raise capital, which attracted investors who began to actively trade the securities. Thus were born the stock exchanges. Today these exchanges need not be physical places, but can be electronic communications networks with their own sets of trading rules binding on participants.[10]

---

[8]Practically, however, a transfer agent in the United States is going to request a medallion guaranteed signature on the stock power in order to prove that the signature by the person making the assignment is not forged. Brokerage houses possess the medallions and will not guarantee a signature unless the transferor has an account with them. Application of the medallion stamp to the power makes the brokerage firm liable in the event of forgery. This requirement ensures that the identity of the signer has been verified and provides a source of recourse to the transferee should there turn out to be a problem with the signature.

[9]The story of the development of these markets is entertaining and informative. See Malcolm Balen, *The Secret History of the South Sea Bubble: The World's First Great Financial Scandal* (HarperCollins 2002), in which one of the world's greatest scientific minds, Sir Isaac Newton, lost a fortune, and Janet Gleeson, *Millionaire: The Philanderer, Gambler and Duelist Who Invented Modern Finance* (Simon & Schuster 1999), a biography of John Law, who popularized paper money issued by a bank; see also John Prebble, *The Darien Disaster*, published in paperback in 1970 by Penguin Books, which documents the story of entrepreneurial Scots who attempted to develop Panama as a trading route in the late seventeenth century—they were wiped out along with the financial capital of Scotland, thereby precipitating the union of Scotland with England in 1707. More than any others, it is really the Dutch to whom we can give credit for the development of modern banking and markets. For a compilation of excellent scholarship on the development of markets, see *The Origin and Development of Financial Markets and Institutions from the Seventeenth Century to the Present*, edited by Jeremy Atack and Larry Neal (Cambridge University Press 2009). For entertaining historical fiction about the Dutch market in the seventeenth century and the London market in the eighteenth century enjoy *The Coffee Trader* and *A Conspiracy of Paper*, both by David Liss and published by Random House.

[10] For information on the development of electronic exchanges and multilateral trading facilities, see Joseph Rosen, *The Electronic Trading Handbook* (Capital Markets Media 2008).

Clearing and settlement is the good delivery securities in return for the good delivery of payment.

Just as with a private sale of securities, the completion of an exchange-based securities transaction must be accompanied by the good delivery of the security in return for the good delivery of payment. This is the classic definition of clearing and settlement. As can be readily understood from the description of the roles of certificates and assignments and transfer agents, the execution, clearing and settlement process consumed a vast amount of paper.[11] The entire market cried out for a new way forward.

---

[11] See David Weiss, *After the Trade Is Made: Processing Securities Transactions* (Penguin Books 2006), which provides a readable description of post-trade processing.

CHAPTER 2

The Growth of Exchanges around the Globe and the Development of Screen-Based Trading

In analyzing the media markets, Marshall McCluhan observed, "The Medium is The Message." The same can be said of exchanges where the medium—electronic trading—is the message. Not unlike the development of new institutions for the clearance and settlement of securities trades discussed in Chapter 3, the seeds for electronic, or screen-based, trading were planted in the 1960s—first with Instinet (founded in 1967) and then with Nasdaq. With the advent of Nasdaq's electronic, screen-based system in 1971, which linked multiple market makers ready to deal at quoted bids and offers, the "technological barrier was broken" and trading was lifted away from the physical confines of a trading floor. London, Singapore, Japan, and various European countries adopted the model in the coming decades. Accelerating as trading technology advanced and the Berlin Wall fell, there has been a proliferation of new exchanges—electronic exchanges—since the late 1980s.[1]

---

[1]The London Stock Exchange went electronic in 1986. For a fulsome description of the development of the Nasdaq market, see *The NASDAQ Handbook, The Stock Market for the Next Hundred Years* (Probus Publishing 1992). Of particular interest to some may be the chapter on the economics of market making by Professor Hans Stoll. In a nutshell, the market maker makes his money by selling at the ask, buying at the bid, and keeping the spread. This is in contradistinction to the specialist system, once hallmark of the New York Stock Exchange, where specialists, assigned to specific stocks, represented customer orders to NYSE members and essentially made money as agents earning fees along the way. However, the specialists were also charged with keeping orderly markets in periods of market disruption. In exchange for this duty, specialists enjoyed an information advantage because they could see all the orders

Although this book is not about advocating the relative merits of investing in developed markets, emerging markets or so-called "Frontier Markets," it is worth noting that the relative market share of the U.S. stock market has been steadily declining over recent years. Presently U.S. stock market shares accounts for roughly 40 percent of world capitalization down from a high of 53 percent as recently as 2004.

Market share is typically measured as a percentage of readily investable shares—the *free float*—as opposed to shares that may be held, for example, by a government. One factor, of course, that has contributed to the enormous growth in emerging and frontier market shares relative to developed markets is the privatization by governments of previously state owned corporations.

Figure 2.1 gives a graphic representation of relative size of global exchanges.

While exchange markets continue to evolve, there are broad themes that can be agreed upon:

- Call auction markets (open outcry exchanges) are all but dead. The Montevideo Stock Exchange, for example, has open outcry only from 4:30 P.M. to 5 P.M. each day while its electronic bourse handles the bulk of trading activity.
- Exchanges have evolved to profit-making enterprises from mutually owned enterprises. The stated reason is the need for capital to develop the electronic technology. Equally plausible as an explanation for the demutualization of exchanges is simply their monetization for the benefit of members (following in the footsteps of the demutualizations of insurance companies and savings and loans).
- Exchanges will continue to link together or merge so they can provide the deepest liquidity and best access to a wide array of financial instruments. The evidence is palpable in the NYSE/Euronext merger,

---

they represented and, as long as they did not take undue advantage of their position, could trade along with customer orders and make money trading for their own accounts. In 2008, the NYSE, under the leadership of Duncan Niederauer, eliminated the old specialist system (and the information advantage they enjoyed) and instead created "Designated Market Makers" with some of the responsibilities specialists used to have. A study performed by the Capital Markets Company revealed that in 1988 stock exchanges existed in 63 countries—26 percent of the world. For perspective, this correlated to 58 percent of the world population and 81 percent of GDP. Less than 20 years later, there were exchanges in 145 countries, close to 60 percent of the world. In two decades, the amount of population serviced by an exchange had grown to 92 percent of the world population and the country coverage represented 99 percent of global GDP.

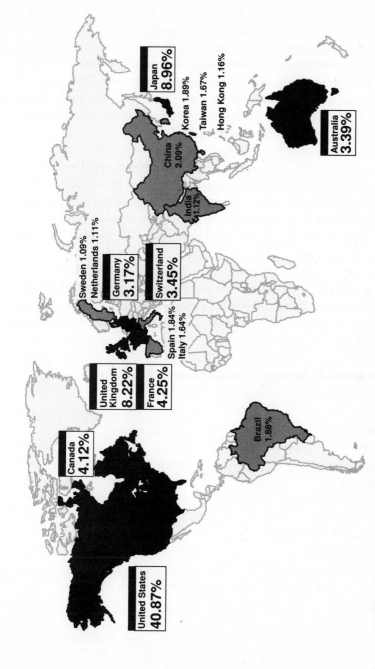

FIGURE 2.1 Percentage of World Stock Market
Source: Standard & Poor's, *World by Numbers,* September 2009.

the Nasdaq/OMX merger and the stated objectives of exchanges from Santiago to Singapore to link together.

■ Enabled by the development in 1992 of the FIX protocol communications network for processing trades, the human trader has been supplanted by algorithms. It is estimated that currently 60 percent of U.S. equity trades are executed using an order management system that, for example, contains an algebraic formula that conditions buy and sell orders in pieces over time in response to various market factors all with the goal of obtaining the best price possible.

Beyond these verities, it remains to be seen which exchanges will survive. A more interesting question, considering the evolution of exchanges, is the need for an exchange to develop, which can support liquidity for alternative investments; that is, illiquid interests in various enterprises not currently listed on an exchange. Surely, the exchange of the future will meet this developing market need.

For perspective, the top 10 exchanges by equity market capitalization as of year-end 2009 are listed next (the grouping is by the World Federation of Stock Exchanges). Table 2.1 is a list (which may be of interest to international investors looking for liquid stocks) of major equity markets with some of their actively traded stocks.

Top 10 Exchanges by Market Capitalization
 1. NYSE Euronext (U.S.)
 2. Tokyo SE
 3. Nasdaq OMX
 4. NYSE Euronext (Europe)
 5. London SE
 6. Shanghai SE
 7. Hong Kong Exchanges
 8. TSX Group
 9. BME Spanish Exchanges
10. BM and FBOVESPA

TABLE 2.1 Major Stock Exchanges with a List of Actively Traded Stocks and Internet Links to Financial Information

Country	Exchange (market cap millions of USD)	Security (by volume)	Financials
Asia/Pacific			
Australia	Australian SE 1650000	OBJ LTD	www.obj.com.au/investor-relations-2
		Monito	www.monitorenergy.com.au/investors/asx_announcements.phtml
		Laguna	www.lagunaresources.com/Investors.html
		Continental Coal	www.conticoal.com/investors
		Rox Res	www.roxresources.com.au/annual_reports.17.html
Bangladesh	Dhaka Stock Exchange Limited 19020.18	SIBL	www.siblbd.com/
		PremBank	www.premierbankltd.com/
		Shnpkr Cer	www.shinepukur.com/
		Bextex Ltd.	www.bextex.net/
		EXIM Bank	www.eximbankbd.com/
China	Shanghai SE2400000	BaoTou Steel	www.btsteel.com/web/index.html
	Shenzhen SE 828700	ShangDong Gold	www.sd-gold.com
		PingAn Insuranc	www.pingan.com/investor/en/index.jsp
		ZhongJin Gold	www.zjgold.com
		Industrial Bank Co	www.cib.com.cn/netbank/en/Investor_Relations
		Vanke	www9.vanke.com/main/defaultEnglish.aspx

(Continued)

TABLE 2.1 (*Continued*)

Country	Exchange (market cap millions of USD)	Security (by volume)	Financials
Hong Kong	Hong Kong Exchanges 2300000	SolarTech Int'l	www.1166hk.com/financials.php
		China Gas Hold	www.chinagasholdings.com.hk/en/investor/results.jsp
		NewSmart Energ	http://newsmartgroup.etnet.com.hk/quote-e.html
		EPI (Holdings)	www.epiholdings.com/reports.shtml
		China ENV RES	http://benefun.etnet.com.hk/quote-e.html
India	Bombay SE 1071938.042	TataSteel	www.tatasteel.com/investors/index.asp
		SBIN	www.statebankofindia.com/user.htm
	National Stock Exchange India 1540000	Reliance	www.ril.com/html/investor/financials.html
		Maruti	www.marutisuzuki.com/investors.aspx
		TataMtrs	http://ir.tatamotors.com
Indonesia	Indonesia SE 269900	Bakrieland	www.bakrieland.com/component/option,com_financialinfo
		Tower Bersama	www.tower-bersama.com
		AsiaInfo Linkage	www.asiainfo.com/investor
		PT Cowl Develop	www.cowelldev.com/cowell/index.php/financials
		PT Bumi Resource	www.bumiresources.com/index.php?option=com_wrapper&Itemid=4

Country	Exchange	Company	Website
Japan	Tokyo SE 3100000	Mizuho	www.mizuho-fg.co.jp/english/investors/index.html
		Mitsub Tk	www.mufg.jp/english/ir/fs/
		Nomura Holdings	www.nomuraholdings.com/investor
		Shinsei BK Ltd	www.shinseibank.com/investors/en/ir/index.html
		Toshiba Corp	www.toshiba.co.jp/about/ir/index.htm
Malaysia	Bursa Malaysia 321400	MMHE Bhd	www.mmhe.com.my/
		Talam	www.talam.com.my/
		KaramCorp	www.karambunaicorp.com/
		HWGB	www.hwgenting.com.my/
		AsiaPac Hld	www.asianpac.com.my/
New Zealand	New Zealand Exchange 54623.106	Telc of NZ	http://investor.telecom.co.nz/phoenix.zhtml?c=91956&p=irol-IRHome
		F&P Health	www.fphcare.com/
		FletchrBld	www.fletcherbuilding.com/investor
		KiwiIncProp	www.kipt.co.nz/
		AuckIndAir	www.aucklandairport.co.nz/Corporate/Investors.aspx
Singapore	Singapore Exchange 419446.633	DBS	www.dbs.com.sg/investor/Pages/default.aspx
		UOB	www.uobgroup.com/investor/index.html
		Keppel	www.kepcorp.com/investorrelations/financialresults.asp
		SporePress	http://sph.listedcompany.com/

(Continued)

TABLE 2.1 (*Continued*)

Country	Exchange (market cap millions of USD)	Security (by volume)	Financials
Sri Lanka	Colombo SE 10839.95991	DialogAxiata	www.dialog.lk/about/investors/financials/
		John Keels Holdings	www.dialog.lk/about/investors/financials/
		Seylan	www.eseylan.com/financial_info.php
		VallibelPwr	www.vallibel-hydro.com/investor_relations/annual_reports.htm
		Erathna	
		Primal Glass	http://glass.piramal.com/corporate/investors-news/financials.html
Taiwan	Taiwan SE Corp. 21218408	UMC	www.umc.com
		YangMing	www.yml.com.tw/
		TaiwanSem	www.tsmc.com
		Wintek	www.wintek.com.tw/
		Polaris Fin	www.pmf.com.tw/
Thailand	The Stock Exchange of Thailand 266831.44937	JAS	www.jasmine.com/jasmineweb/html/index.asp
		N-Park	www.naturalpark.co.th/EN/main.html
		SuperBlock	www.superblockthailand.com/indexb.html
		BTS Group	www.tanayong.co.th/index.php
		G-Steel	www.g-steel.com/en/home.asp
South Korea	Korea Exchange 720548.2425	Kia Motors	www.kmcir.com/eng/index.aspx
		Hynix Semi	www.hynix.com/gl/ir/index.jsp?menuNo=3&m=0&s=0

Region	Exchange	Company	URL
Europe			
Austria	Wiener Börse 109395.3	LG Display	www.lgdisplay.com/homeContain/jsp/eng/inv/inv000_j_e.jsp
		HyundaiMot	http://worldwide.hyundai.com/
		HyundMobis	www.mobis.co.kr/eng/
		DeutscheBank	http://deutsche-boerse.com
		Raiffeisen Centrobank	www.rcb.at/Annual_Reports.557.0.html
		Erste Group Bank AG	www.erstegroup.com
		Morgan Stanley	www.morganstanley.com/
		Credit Suisse	www.credit-suisse.com
		Reinet Investments	www.reinet.com/investor-relations.html
Belgium/Lux	Luxembourg Stock Exchange 396653.6 NYSE Euronext	Intercultures	www.socfinal.lu/Public/Micro_site.php?ID=904
		Socfinasia	www.socfinal.lu/Public/Micro_site.php?ID=904
		Luxempart	www.luxempart.lu/DisplayPage.asp?pid=338
		SESG	www.ses.com/ses/siteSections/investorRelations/
Czech Republic	Prague Stock Exchange 75853.20	Erste Group Bank	www.erstegroup.com
		CEZ	www.cez.cz/en/investors.html
		Komercni Banka	www.kb.cz/en/about-the-bank/investor_relations/index.shtml
		Telefonica O2 C.R	www.o2.cz/osobni/en/3032-investor_relations/
		NWR	www.newworldresources.eu/nwr/pages/home

(Continued)

TABLE 2.1 (*Continued*)

Country	Exchange (market cap millions of USD)	Security (by volume)	Financials
Denmark	Nasdaq OMX Group 817222.8	Vestas Wind Systems	www.vestas.com/en
		Danske Bank	www.danskebank.com/en-uk
		Novo Nordisk B	www.novonordisk.com/investors/
		FLsmidth & Co.	www.flsmidth.com/en-US/Investor+Relations
		Nordea Bank	www.nordea.com/Investor+Relations/50892.html
Finland	Nasdaq OMX Group 817222.8	Nokia	www.nokia.com
		Stora Enso R	www.storaenso.com/investors
		Outokumpu Oyj	www.outokumpu.com/Investors/
		TeliaSonera	www.teliasonera.com/About-TeliaSonera/Financial-information/
		UPM-Kynmmene Oyj	http://investors.upm.com/
France	NYSE Euronext 2869393.1	Alcatel	www.alcatel-lucent.com/wps/portal/!ut
		ArcelOrmittal	www.arcelormittal.com/index.php?lang=en&page=476
		RBS	www.investors.rbs.com/news/releasedetail022609.cfm
		Vodafone	www.vodafone.com/static/annual_report09/index.html

Country	Exchange	Company	URL
UK	London Stock Exchange 1703249.75	Barclays	http://group.barclays.com
		BP PLC	www.bp.com/investortools.do?categoryId=1458&contentId=2014277
		Lloyds Bkg	www.lloydsbankinggroup.com
Germany	Deutsche Börse 842618.54	Siemens	www.siemens.com/investor/en/index.htm
		Daimler	www.daimler.com/investor-relations/en
		DeutTelkm	www.telekom.com/dtag/cms/content/dt
		Bayer	www.investor.bayer.com/en
		DeutBank	www.arcandor.com/en/225.asp
Greece	Athens Exchange 834526.78	NatBkG	www.nbg.gr
		Alpha Bk	www.alpha.gr/page/default.asp?la=2&id=3002
		Bk Piraeus	www.piraeusbank.gr
		OPAP	www.opap.gr
		EFGEbk	www.efgbank.com
Ireland	Irish Stock Exchange 38814.019	BkofIreland	www.bankofireland.com/investor/index.html
		Kerry Group	www.kerrygroup.com/investor_index.asp
		PaddyPower	www.paddypowerplc.com/cms/investor_fact_sheet
		CRH PLC	www.crh.ie/crhcorp/ir/
		Ryanair	www.ryanair.com

(Continued)

TABLE 2.1 (*Continued*)

Country	Exchange (market cap millions of USD)	Security (by volume)	Financials
Italy	Borsa Italiana 414923.06	UniCred	www.unicreditgroup.eu/ucg-static
		IntSPaolo	
		Telecmltal	www.telecomitalia.it/cgi-bin
		Enel	www.enel.it/azienda/en
		Eni	www.eni.it/en_IT
Netherlands	NYSE Euronext	Arcelor Mittal	www.arcelormittal.com/index.php?lang=en&page =411
		ING	www.ing.com/group/investorrelations.jsp?& menopt=ivr&menopt=ivr&pipe;ivr
		Millennium BCP	www.millenniumbcp.pt/pubs/en/investorrelations/
		Alcatel-Lucent	www.alcatel-lucent.com/wps/portal/investors
		AXA	www.axa.com/en/investor/
Norway	NASDAQ OMX Nordic 419482.92	Vestas	h www.vestas.com/en/investor.aspx
		Ericsson	www.ericsson.com/ericsson/investors/
	Oslo Børs 227220.00	Sandvik	www.sandvik.com/
		Volvo	www.volvogroup.com/GROUP/GLOBAL/EN-GB/INVESTORS/Pages/investor_relations.aspx

Poland	Warsaw Stock Exchange 81414.88	KGHM	www.kghm.pl/index.dhtml?category_id=3117&lang=en
		PKOBP	www.bankowy.pl
		Polish Telecom	www.tp-ir.pl/?page=investors_key
		PEKAO	www.pekao.com.pl/information_for_investors
Portugal	NYSE Euronext	Millennium BCP	www.millenniumbcp.pt/pubs/en/investorrelations/
		ING	www.ing.com
		Alcatel-Lucent	www.alcatel-lucent.com
		RDSA	www.shell.com/home/content/investor/
		Aegon	www.aegon.com/en/Home/Investors/
Spain	Spanish Exchanges (BME) 835958.54	XAMXL	www.americamovil.com/index_eng.htm
		XBBDC	www.banorte.com/portal/banorte.portal?_nfpb=true&_pageLabel=pagePersonalSolution&solutionId=112&trends=17
		XCMIG	http://cemig.infoinvest.com.br/?language=ptb
		XCOP	www.copel.com/hpcopel/ri/

(Continued)

TABLE 2.1 (*Continued*)

Country	Exchange (market cap millions of USD)	Security (by volume)	Financials
Sweden	Oslo Børs 227220.00	SCF Technologies	www.scf-technologies.com/default.asp?id=233
	Nasdaq OMX Group 109509.00	Life Cycle Pharma	www.lcpharma.com/investors.cfm
		CHEMM	www.chemometec.com/en-GB/IR.aspx
		Schaumann Group	www.schaumanngroup.com/investorrelations
		Topsil	www.topsil.com/374
Switzerland	SIX Swiss Exchange 832356.10	Actelion	www1.actelion.com/en/investors/index.page?
		UBS	https://clientlogin.ibb.ubs.com/login?_URI=aHR0cDovL2NsaWVudHBvcnRhbC5C5pYmluddWJzLmNvbS9wb3J0YWwvXXwvaW5kZXguaHRtbD8BhZ2U9aG9tZ%3D%3D
		Adecco	www.adecco.com/INVESTORRELATIONS/Pages/InvestorRelations.aspx
		Credit Suisse	https://emagazine.credit-suisse.com/app/article/index.cfm?fuseaction=OpenArticle&aoid=291283&coid=162&lang=EN
		Julius Baer	www.juliusbaer.com/htm/671/en/Media-%26-Investors.htm

Americas			
Argentina	Bolsa de Comercio de Buenos Aires 45700	Petrobras	www.petrobras.com.br/en/about-us/profile/
		Banco Hipotecario	www.hipotecario.com.ar/default.asp
		Grupo Financiero Galicia	www.gfgsa.com/
Brazil	BM&FBOVESPA 1337213.10	Vale SA	www.vale.com
		Petrobas PF	www.petrobras.com.br/pt
		OGX Pertoleo	www.ebx.com.br
		Itau Unibanco	www.itau-unibanco.com.br/ri
		Usiminas	www.usiminas.com/br
Canada	TSX Group 1847103.09	TeckResB	www.teck.com
		Suncor En	www.suncor.com
		RylBkC	www.rbcroyalbank.com
		Eastern Platinum	www.eastplats.com
		Equinox Minerals	www.equinoxminerals.com
Mexico	Mexican Exchange 352000	CemxCPO	www.cemex.com/ic/ic_lp.asp
		AmerMvl	http://marvel.com/company/index.htm
		GMexico	www.gmexico.com/
		Walmex	http://phx.corporate-ir.net/phoenix.zhtml?c=130639&p=irol-irhome
		Grupo Fin Banorte	www.esmas.com/televisainversionistas/eng/

(Continued)

TABLE 2.1 (*Continued*)

Country	Exchange (market cap millions of USD)	Security (by volume)	Financials
USA			
NYSE	NYSE Euronext (US) 9739784.54	Citigroup	www.citibank.com/citi/fin/
		BankAm	http://investor.bankofamerica.com/phoenix.zhtml?c=71595&p=irol-irhome
		GenElectr	www.ge.com/investors/index.html
		Exxon	www.exxonmobil.com/Corporate/
NASDAQ	NASDAQ OMX 2811980.17	Microsoft	www.microsoft.com/
		Intel Corp	www.intel.com/
		Cisco	http://investor.cisco.com/
		Oracle	www.oracle.com/corporate/investor_relations/index.html
		Comcast A	www.cmcsk.com/
Middle East/Africa			
Egypt	Egyptian Exchange (EGX) 78150	Egyptian for Tourism Resorts	http://investing.businessweek.com/research/stocks/snapshot/snapshot.asp?ticker=EGTS:EY
		Orascom Telecom Holding	http://otelecom.com/Investor_Relations/Annual Reports.aspx
		Arab Cotton Ginning	http://investing.businessweek.com/research/stocks/snapshot/snapshot.asp?ticker=ACGC:EY

Country	Company	URL
	Upper Egypt Contracting	http://investing.businessweek.com/research/stocks/snapshot/snapshot.asp?ticker=UEGC:EY
	Arab Polvara Spinning & Weaving Co.	http://in.reuters.com/finance/stocks/overview?symbol=APSW.CA&exchange=EGC
Iran Tehran Stock Exchange (TSE) 72000	Iran Zinc Mines	http://en.izmdc.com/index.aspx?siteid=82&pageid=213
	Karafarin Bank	www.karafarinbank.com/Earchive/EarchiveE/Itemlist.asp?PareneId=6
	Sadra	www.sadra.ir/
	Arak M. Mfg	
	Mapna Group	www.mapna.com/En/default.aspx
Israel Tel Aviv Stock Exchange (TASE) 189000	Israel Discount Bank	http://phx.corporate-ir.net/phoenix.zhtml?c=166348&p=irol-IRHome
	Israel Chemicals Ltd.	www.icl-group.com/investorinformation/Pages/StockInformation.aspx
	Leumi	http://english.leumi.co.il/LEPrivate/Investor_Relations/6254/
	Bezeq	http://ir.bezeq.co.il/phoenix.zhtml?c=159870&p=irol-IRHome
	Teva Pharmaceutical	www.tevapharm.com/financial/

(Continued)

TABLE 2.1 (*Continued*)

Country	Exchange (market cap millions of USD)	Security (by volume)	Financials
Jordan	Amman Stock Exchange (ASE) 29590	Al Ahlia Enterprises	http://investing.businessweek.com/businessweek/research/stocks/snapshot/snapshot.asp?ticker=ABLA:JR
		Arab Bank	www.arabbank.com/en/investorrelation.aspx
		Specialized Jordanian Investments	http://investing.businessweek.com/research/stocks/snapshot/snapshot.asp?ticker=SIJC:JR
		Al Tajamouat for Touristic Projects Company	http://altajamouategypt.com/doc/group_touristic.htm
		Jordan Emirates Insurance Company P.S.C	http://joemirates.com/financial
Kuwait	Kuwait Stock Exchange (KSE) 127890	Investors Holding Group	http://investing.businessweek.com/research/stocks/snapshot/snapshot.asp?ticker=INVESTOR:KK
		National Ranges Company K.S.C.C	www.mayadeen.com/about.html
		International Financial Advisors	www.ifakuwait.com/ir_repors.html

Country	Company	URL
	Abyaar Real Estate Investment Co. K.S.C.C.	http://abyaar.com/reports.html
	Alsalam Group Holding Co. K.S.C.C.	www.alsalamholding.com/annual_reports.html
Lebanon Beirut Stock Exchange (BSE) 12210	Solidere A Byblos Bank	www.solidere.com/invest/types.html www.byblosbank.com.lb/newscenter/annual_report/index.shtml
	Solidere B Holcim Liban	www.solidere.com/invest/types.html www.holcim.com.lb/LB/FR/id/-20064/mod/6_2_1/page/publication_second_list.html
Libya Libyan Stock Exchange (LYX) 2350	Sahara Bank	http://www.saharabank.com.ly/en/pid883/corporate.html
	Wahda Bank	http://www.wahdabank.org/english/reports/2007.pdf
	Libya Trade & Development Bank	
	Al-Jomhouriya Bank	
	United Insurance Company	

(Continued)

TABLE 2.1 (*Continued*)

Country	Exchange (market cap millions of USD)	Security (by volume)	Financials
Qatar	Qatar Exchange (DSM) 50000	Vodafone Qatar	www.vodafone.com.qa/go/en/investorrelations
		Masraf Al Rayan	www.alrayan.com/english/index.php?page=press-releases
		Al Khalij Holding Company	www.alkhalijiholding.com/Investor.aspx?CatId=9
		Mazaya Qatar	www.mazayaqatar.com/en/index.asp
		Barwa Real Estate Company	www.barwa.com.qa/english/eng.aspx
Saudi Arabia	Bahrain Stock Exchange (BSE) 16990	Khaleeji Commercial Bank	http://khcb.info/en/AboutKHCB.aspx
		Seef Properties B.S.C.	www.bahrainstock.com/downloads/Financials/SEEF.pdf
		Al Salam Bank	www.alsalambank.net/html/report.html
		BBK	www.bbkonline.com/InvestorRelations/Pages/InvestorRelations.aspx
		Bahrain National Holding Co.	http://bnhgroup.com/

Location	Exchange	Company	URL
Abu Dhabi	Abu Dhabi Securities Exchange (ADX)79400	Emirates Telecommunications Corp.	www.gulfbase.com/site/interface/Company ProfileSummary.aspx?c=448
		National Bank of Abu Dhabi	http://nbad.com/investor/
		First Gulf Bank	www.fgb.ae/en/home/financialhighlights.asp#0
		Abu Dhabi Commercial Bank	http:/adcbindia.com/
		Abu Dhabi National Energy Company	www.taqa.ae/en/annual_reports.html
Dubai	Dubai Financial Market (DFM) 360000	Deyaar Development	www.deyaar.ae/Eng/Invester/Default.aspx?PageID =CD3B4203FD5E7CD13AC4
		Ekttitab	www.gulfbase.com/site/interface/CompanyProfile Summary.aspx?c=590
		Emaar	www.emaar.com/index.aspx?page=investorrelations
		Arabtec	
		Almadina	www.almadina.com/investment_services/ investment_services.asp
		Arabtec	

CHAPTER 3

The Paper Crunch and Development of New Institutions

J ust as exchanges started to evolve in the 1960s so did clearance and settlement systems. All the paper moving about among brokers and transfer agents crushed the U.S. securities settlement system in the late 1960s.[1] Former Secretary of the U.S. Treasury and former CEO of Merrill Lynch, Donald T. Regan, described Wall Street as caught in a "paper blizzard" (see Figure 3.1). The New York Stock Exchange (NYSE) restricted trading periods, and brokerage firms ran three shifts a day to try to keep up. The result of the blizzard was a dramatic change in recording securities transactions and ownership.

In order to understand the development of modern clearing systems and the securities intermediaries that custody securities (a securities intermediary is an entity that stands between the investor and the issuer of the securities—it could be a bank or a broker-dealer or a combination of both), one has to first understand the following: (1) the concept of a trust, (2) a central securities depository (CSD), (3) multilateral netting, and (4) a central counterparty (CCP).

THE TRUST

A trust allows the legal title of a thing to rest with one party but be subject to the direction of another party for the benefit a third party. The time-honored

---

[1] In fact, it was once a rule that all members of the New York Stock Exchange (NYSE) had to have offices below Chambers Street in New York in order to facilitate delivery of securities. In the 1960s, trading reached such volumes that some firms could simply not keep up and a number of firms failed in the late 1960s and early 1970s, precipitating the Securities Investor Protection Corporation; see Chapter 15. For a vivid account of Wall Street in the 1960s refer to John Brooks, *The Go-Go Years: The Drama and Crashing Finale of Wall Street's Bullish*

FIGURE 3.1   1969 Apollo 11 Ticker Tape Parade in the Wall Street District of New York. The paper seen in the background is shredded paper from securities transactions.
Source: Courtesy of NASA

example is the English knight who gives the title to his land to his friend to hold in trust for his wife and children in the event that he is killed in battle. Trust law is a unique feature of English common law. Unless adopted by legislation, the concept of a trust is unknown in many jurisdictions.[2] For

---

60's (Weybright & Talley 1973), which chronicles the failure in the 1960s of once-storied firms like Hayden, Stone, F.I. du Pont, and Goodbody & Co.

[2]The commercial laws that govern the global securities markets fall principally in two camps: civil law and common law. In its simplest terms, civil law is driven by statutes, codes, and decrees. Common law is often referred to as *judge-made law*. Common law derives from judges' decisions evolving to meet changing circumstances and the dictates of fairness. Starting with the development of the Field Code by Justice David Field in New York in the nineteenth century, the United States and other common law jurisdictions, like England and Britain's former colonies and territories, have been codifying their laws. The most notable examples in the United States are the "Uniform Commercial Code" and the "Federal Bankruptcy Code." Civil law jurisdictions, by statute or decree, have adopted for special purposes perhaps the most famous and elastic creation of the common law—The Trust. As discussed, this has been an important development in the clearing, settlement and custody of securities.

From crusaders, the idea of the trust was born.

example, a Royal Decree was required in Luxembourg to establish the legal basis for Clearstream. Similarly, a statute was required in Belgium for the creation of Euroclear.

CENTRAL SECURITIES DEPOSITORY

A CSD is a utility that holds securities. In many cases, the CSD holds these securities in trust for another, usually a member which is a bank or broker (which in turn holds in trust for its client).[3] Brokers and banks use the CSD as a central place to house transferable certificates that they trade with

---

[3]Exceptions to the CSD as trustee model include VPC in Sweden and CREST in the United Kingdom where the members of the CSD, rather than the CSD, are the legal owners. In the case of Clearstream Banking Frankfurt, the German CSD, and Euroclear France, the French CSD, these CSDs hold the securities, but do not own them. Ownership is conferred on the holder of the account at the CSD member. In some circumstances (the CHESS system in Australia being the notable example) individuals hold their securities directly with the CSD.

each other. Securities held with a CSD are not claimable by creditors of the CSD in the event of the insolvency of the CSD, so the certificates are safe there. Typically, a CSD member is a bank or brokerage firm. If it is a bank or broker based in a common law jurisdiction, trust law and its protection from creditors will apply.[4] If the bank or broker is located in a civil law jurisdiction or other legal regime, care must be taken to examine the creditworthiness of the custodian and the legal status of securities custodied at the CSD through the bank or broker in the event of the bank's or broker's insolvency. Selection of a creditworthy custodian in foreign markets is therefore of paramount concern to the cross-border investor.

NETTING

One of the benefits of a CSD is that the centralization of the securities allows members to settle securities trades on a net basis. This eliminates the need to move securities and cash physically from member to member, all such movements being made electronically on a net basis. Netting is a fairly basic concept to understand. Examine the example shown in Figure 3.2.

Before netting, A owes B $10; B owes C $10; C owes D $5; D owes A $2; and D owes B $3. If all four parties were to pay each other, then five transactions would need to take place. With the application of netting among the four parties, a different result occurs. Follow the chart. Since B owes C $10, A might as well just pay C directly. Since C owes D $5—but D owes B $3, then C might as well pay B directly and eliminate the needless paperwork. D also owes A $2, which can be deducted from the amount A owes C. Netted down, C pays B $3 and A pays C $8. Instead of five

---

[4]In the United States the general creditors of a bank, in the event of the bank's insolvency, have no right to call on securities held by the bank on behalf of its customers. This is why some think custody of securities at a bank is safer than broker-dealer custody because brokers, under defined circumstances outlined in Chapters 8 and 9, can use customer securities in their business, that is, lend those securities to others or pledge them. In the event of a broker's insolvency some fear that loaned or pledged securities might not be returned by the broker's counterparty or the insolvent broker will struggle to get them back. Just as FDIC insurance mitigates the risk of bank insolvency for a bank depositor so too does SIPC insurance mitigate risk of a broker's insolvency for the broker-dealer customer; see Chapter 15. It is interesting to note that in Holland, in order to prevent bank creditors from getting at customer securities in the event of a Dutch bank's insolvency, banks hold securities in a legally separate affiliated company in order to make clear those securities cannot be attached by creditors in the event of the Dutch bank's insolvency.

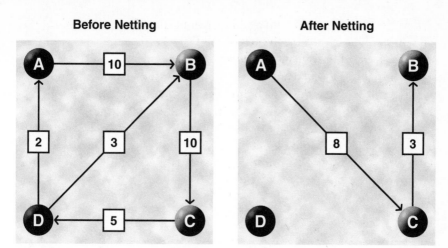

FIGURE 3.2 The Benefits of Netting

transactions and people running around delivering paper to each other, just two movements are needed. The operational advantage is obvious. This is why advanced securities markets have implemented netting as an efficient means of improving clearing and settlement of securities.

CENTRAL COUNTERPARTIES

The answer to the legal problem that arises if one party becomes insolvent before netting or before settlement takes place is the central counterparty. A central counterparty, or CCP, negates this risk by the CCP's becoming the seller to every buyer and the buyer to every seller. Stated another way, each contract among market counterparties is made new again with the CCP. This is called *novation*. Thus, the CCP becomes liable to each and every trade. The CCP mitigates this risk by calling for margin[5] from each participant in the CCP system. Ultimately, the risk of insolvency of any one CCP participant is spread among all participants if the margin and other security obtained by the CCP are exhausted.

---

[5]Margin is an amount of liquid collateral pledged to a lender (see Chapter 8). In this case, it is the CCP that is the lender because it settles a trade without having yet received securities or payment from the participant member.

CHAPTER 4

Central Counterparties and Depositories

In the sections that follow, the three major central securities depositories are described at some length. This provides a good picture of their operations from which can be gleaned the general features of central counterparties (CCPs) and central securities depositories (CSDs) the world over. A complete list of exchanges and their depositories is found in Chapter 5.

THE DEPOSITORY TRUST AND CLEARING CORPORATION

As the largest of the CCPs and CSDs, the Depository Trust & Clearing Corporation (DTCC) custodied more than $27 trillion worth of securities and cleared and settled $455 trillion worth of transactions in 2008. With principal offices in New York, DTCC comprises the Depository Trust Company (DTC; the CSD) and a number of product-specific clearing corporations (the CCPs). These CCPs are the National Securities Clearing Corporation (NSCC), the Fixed Income Clearing Corporation (FICC) and the Emerging Markets Clearing Corporation (EMCC) for stock, bonds and emerging markets, respectively. A distinguishing feature of DTCC is that it is mutually owned by members of the market—the banks and brokers that participate in it. DTCC is not designed to be a profit-making enterprise. In this regard, this business model differs from, for example, the German model, where the exchange also owns the CSD and CCP and clearing and settlement fees enhance the profitability of the affiliated exchange. Most Asian exchanges follow the German business model.[1]

The basic premise of DTCC and other similar industry-created and -owned entities is to immobilize securities in a central location and to allow participants to net trade settlement multilaterally.

Physical stock and bond certificates are deposited at DTC, similar to how you might deposit cash at a bank. In fact, DTC is a limited purpose bank. Again similar to a bank, the depositor can see what it has on deposit by logging in to DTC's system. Holding securities at a central location allows DTC participants to deliver and receive shares electronically via DTC's "banking" system while the shares never leave DTC's vault. This immobilization allows DTC participants to settle trades and process customer account transfers efficiently.

DTC holds the deposited securities in its name (nominally, CEDE & Co., which stands for Central Depository). When a stock pays a dividend or a bond pays interest, the dividend-interest payer pays these funds to DTC, which in turn credits the depositor of the securities. This process has eliminated the need for paying agents to issue hundreds of thousands of checks to individual certificate holders. DTC also has created processes to submit shares for tender offers electronically, eliminating another manual process. For securities lending transactions, DTC keeps track of shares borrowed and loaned. When a dividend is paid on securities on loan, DTC will credit the dividend to the lender and take the dividend money from the borrower. This "income tracking" process also reduces exposure between lending participants.

One of the most critical efficiency-enhancing developments was the creation of NSCC's Continuous Net Settlement (CNS). Brokers that trade with other brokers electronically submit all their trades to CNS for comparison with the other brokers. If all the material trade facts match before noon on T+2, (the trade date plus two business days) the trades are accepted by CNS for multilateral net settlement. Multilateral netting allows each broker to combine all its buys and sells and net the shares and the money. By doing so, on settlement date (currently, the trade date plus three business days), a broker-dealer would have a single delivery or receive obligation and would receive or pay the net money of all the combined trades. Once compared,

---

[1]The evolution of DTCC is a tale in itself. DTCC grew from the NYSE Stock Clearing Corporation, to the failed Central Certificate Service, to the Depository Trust Company, which then merged with the National Securities Clearing Corporation in 1999.

the broker-dealer no longer worries about settlement with the original trading counterparty and instead owes or receives shares and money to or from CNS. If a broker-dealer is unable to make delivery to CNS of any of its obligations, CNS charges the broker-dealer the market value of the undelivered shares as of the day settlement would have occurred. Likewise, if CNS is unable to make delivery to a broker, CNS credits that broker with the market value. This marking to market balances the risk associated with the unsettled shares. And for ease of processing, CNS settlements occur within DTC.

As noted earlier, other central clearing facilities have been created that specialize in other types of securities such as U.S. government debt, mortgage-backed securities, and municipal bonds and unit investment trusts.

In recent years, DTCC has expanded its product offering to include over-the-counter (OTC) derivatives, mutual funds, insurance and retirement products, and Omgeo, an institutional post-trade presettlement comparison service.

EUROCLEAR

Euroclear is a securities settlement system. Like DTCC, it is also a limited purpose bank. Unlike DTCC, it does not operate a CCP like NSCC. Formed in 1968, Euroclear enables its members (through their own accounts in Euroclear) to settle securities transactions by moving securities free of payment or against cash (delivery versus payment or DVP). Euroclear is an international settlement system in that it does not support a particular domestic securities market but supports the settlement of the securities issued in a variety of jurisdictions and under a variety of laws.

Its members are banks, financial institutions or securities houses. They must meet certain criteria for admission to the Euroclear system. These include (a) financial resources, (b) operational capability, and (c) projected settlement volumes.

Euroclear members instruct the settlement of transactions and make inquiries of Euroclear as to their holdings by means of Euroclear's proprietary interface (Euclid) or by using the Society for World Interbank Financial Telecommunication (SWIFT) network. Euclid is available only to Euroclear members. Only Euroclear members can access Euroclear using SWIFT.

Euroclear Bank does not currently disclose the admission criteria for securities, but these are likely to require that (a) a security is freely transferable, (b) interests in it are capable of electronic settlement, and (c) each unit in a security (as denoted by the ISIN—see below) is fungible with every other such unit.

Securities are delivered either (a) in the local market to the local Euroclear depositary (typically, a local bank) for that market or (b) to a depositary appointed by Euroclear Bank for the specific type of instrument. (Euroclear operates a network of depositaries to hold securities for it.) Once the relevant securities are placed in the depositary, Euroclear Bank holds the securities locally in its own name (or that of its nominee). Against this holding, Euroclear then reflects in its books a securities interest under Belgian law on the relevant member's account.

In addition to operating a network of local depositary agent banks, Euroclear also has links to other security settlement systems and, by opening an account in its own name in those settlement systems, can also hold securities in the local market.

Where securities are delivered in the local market to a Euroclear agent bank, this may be effected by electronic means (where securities, or interest in securities, have been dematerialized) or by the delivery of certificates, particularly for bearer instruments. Typically for certificates of deposit, which generally are negotiable bearer instruments, a certificate will be delivered to the local depository. Where the entire issue of a security is delivered into Euroclear (all the units are represented by a single ISIN), frequently a single certificate (a so-called *global* or *jumbo* certificate) will be delivered into the Euroclear system. Global certificates are often issued solely for the purpose of being deposited in this manner in order to support electronic settlement in Euroclear or in another system.

ISINs

Where securities are already in issue in the local market, they will usually bear the international securities identification number (ISIN) attributed in that jurisdiction. Where securities are first delivered or issued into Euroclear (as is the case with most Eurobonds), Euroclear will itself usually issue the ISIN bearing the prefix "XS."[2]

---

[2]In the United States and Canada, the alphanumeric identifier is known as a CUSIP. In the United Kingdom and Ireland, the identifier is the SEDOL.

ACCESS TO INFORMATION REGARDING EUROCLEAR SECURITIES

Euroclear Bank has an informative website, but it does not provide details of securities eligible for settlement in Euroclear either on the website or by any other generally available mechanism. Euroclear members can obtain this information through the Euclid interface or by using the SWIFT network, which is open to banks and other financial institutions. (Other financial services companies are only able to obtain this information through their settlement agents with Euroclear membership.)

It should be noted that the CREST system (as described in the next section), which is owned by Euroclear Bank, does provide through its website details of securities that are eligible to settle in CREST. This will include depositary receipts, which are English law interests in international securities.

CREST

CREST is legally five systems. It acts separately as the national CSD for the United Kingdom, Ireland, Isle of Man, Jersey, and Guernsey. The predominant CREST system is the CREST United Kingdom system. It commenced operations in July 1997 following concerns that the U.K. settlement infrastructure was out of date and after the failure of the London Stock Exchange's Taurus system, which was intended to introduce electronic settlements to the U.K. market. CREST is now operated by Euroclear (United Kingdom and Ireland) Limited. CREST is a direct holding system, which means the account holder establishes legal title by reference to a register of title of which, for U.K. securities (equities, U.K. government bonds or *gilts* as well as certain money market instruments), is effected on a register maintained as part of the CREST system. In Ireland, to record transactions CREST transmits an electronic message, which causes a registrar appointed by the Irish issuer to update its register and title.

CREST is also unusual in that it supports direct membership by individuals (but see also systems like CHESS in Australia and VPC in Sweden where such membership is widespread). Thus, an individual may open an account in CREST in his name and establish legal title to a security based solely on CREST's electronic records. CREST does not immobilize securities in some account at another CSD or in an agent bank, nor does it immobilize securities in paper form.

Securities and cash may only be moved in CREST on the basis of a properly authenticated dematerialized instruction, or PADI. Only a CREST member (or its duly appointed agent called a CREST *sponsor*) using a specific communications process may instruct a movement of cash or securities in CREST. Where payment is made in pounds sterling or in Euros, funds move through the accounts held at the Bank of England or the Central Bank of Ireland, respectively. Settlement in U.S. dollars is effected by settlement banks in commercial bank funds. A feature of the CREST system is that participants can choose from a number of payment banks to extend credit to them or to effect payments on their behalf.

The Santiago Stock Exchange. The exchange is electronic today. In the background is a picturesque reminder of days when transactions were recorded by clerks on a chalkboard.

CHAPTER 5

Major Worldwide Exchanges and Their Associated Depositories, and Practical Tips on Execution, Clearance, and Custody in Various Regions around the Globe

Deutsche Börse

This chapter lists the major exchanges of the world along with their associated central clearing counterparties and central securities depositories. Practical tips about trading, settlement, and custody in certain regions are also provided. Last, so-called "passenger markets" are explained. Passenger markets are found in many countries and, as the case study in this chapter highlights, can pose problems for the unwary if accounts in those countries are not established correctly.

PRACTICAL COMMENTARY CONCERNING TRADING, CLEARING, AND CUSTODY IN EUROPE

TABLE 5.1 Europe

Country	Exchanges	Central Securities Depository	Central Counterparty
Austria	Wiener Boerse AG (VSE)	Oesterreichische Kontrollbank AG (OeKB)	CCP.A
Belgium	Euronext Brussels	Euroclear Belgium	LCH.Clearnet SA
Bulgaria	Bulgaria Stock Exchange-Sofia (BSE)	Central Depository AD (CDAD)	None
Croatia	Zagreb Stock Exchange (ZSE)	Central Depository & Clearing Company Inc. (CDCC) of Croatia	Central Depository & Clearing Company Inc. (CDCC) of Croatia
Czech Republic	Prague Stock Exchange	The Czech Republic does not have a Central Depository. Stredisko Cennych Papiru serves as a central securities registry	None

TABLE 5.1 (*Continued*)

Country	Exchanges	Central Securities Depository	Central Counterparty
Denmark	OMX Nordic Exchange, Copenhagen	Vaerdipapircentralen (VP) (The Danish Securities Centre)	None
Estonia	OMX Nordic Exchange, Tallin	Estonian Central Securities Depository (ECSD)	None
Finland	OMX Nordic Exchange, Helsinki	Suomen Arvopaperikeskus Oy (Finnish Central Securities Depository Ltd.)	None
France	Euronext Paris	Euroclear France	LCH.Clearnet SA
Germany	Börsen AG Boerse Berlin Equiduct Trading Boerse Düsseldorf Boerse Munich Boerse Stuttgart Deutsche Boerse Hamburger Boerse	Clearstream Banking AG, Frankfurt (CBF)	Eurex Clearing AG
Greece	Athens Exchange (ATHEX)	Hellenic Exchanges SA (HELEX)	None
Hungary	Budapest Stock Exchange (BSE)	Kozponti Elszamolohaz es Ertektar Zrt (KELER)	KELER KSZF
Iceland	OMX Nordic Exchange, Iceland	Icelandic Securities Depository Limited (ISD)	None
Ireland	Irish Stock Exchange (ISE)	Euroclear UK & Ireland Ltd.	Eurex Clearing AG
Italy	Borsa Italiana	Monte Titoli SPA	Cassa di Compensazione e Garanzia S.p.A.

(*Continued*)

TABLE 5.1   (*Continued*)

Country	Exchanges	Central Securities Depository	Central Counterparty
Latvia	OMX Nordic Exchange, Riga	Latvian Central Depository (LCD)	None
Lithuania	OMX Nordic Exchange, Vilnius	Lietuvous Centrinis Vertybiniv Popieriv Depozitoriumas (Central Securities Depository of Lithuania)	None
Luxembourg	Luxembourg Stock Exchange (BdL)	Clearstream Banking SA, Luxembourg	LCH.Clearnet SA
Netherlands	Euronext Amsterdam N.V.	Euroclear Nederland	LCH.Clearnet SA
Norway	Oslo Børs	Verdipapirsentralen (The Norwegian Central Securities Depository)	Oslo Clearing ASA
Poland	Warsaw Stock Exchange (WSE)	Krajowy Depozyt Papierow Wartosciowych SA (National Depository of Securities)	None
Portugal	Euronext Lisbon	INTERBOLSA— Sociedade Gestora de Sistemas de Liquidacao e de Sistemas Centralizados de Valores Mobiliarios, SA	LCH.Clearnet SA
Romania	Bucharest Stock Exchange (BSE)	Depozitarul Central (CSD)	None

TABLE 5.1 (*Continued*)

Country	Exchanges	Central Securities Depository	Central Counterparty
Russia	Moscow Interbank Currency Exchange (MICEX) RTS Stock Exchange Saint Petersburg Stock Exchange (SPBEX)	Depository Clearing Corp (DCC) and National Depository Center (NDC)	No official central counterparty. RTS Clearing Center acts as CCP in certain situations.
Slovak Republic	Bratislava Stock Exchange (BSSE)	Centralny depozitar cennych papierov (CSD)	None
Slovenia	Ljubljana Stock Exchange (LJSE)	KDD—Centralna klirinsko depotna druzba d.d. (KDD)	None
Spain	Bolsa de Madrid (main exchange) Bolsa de Bilbao Bolsa de Barcelona Bolsa de Valencia	IBERCLEAR	None
Sweden	OMX Nordic Exchange Stockholm AB	Euroclear Sweden AB	SIX X-Clear and EuroCCP
Switzerland	Swiss Exchange (SWX)	SIX SIS AG (SIS)	SIX X-Clear AG, LCH.Clearnet SA
United Kingdom	London Stock Exchange (LSE)	Euroclear UK & Ireland Ltd.	London Clearing House (LCH)

Although most exchanges quote in dollars and cents (or equivalent in currency), United Kingdom, South African, and Israeli stocks quote in local equivalents to cents. So if British Petroleum has a price in the United Kingdom of GBP 4.75, it would be quoted on the exchange (and among traders) as 475 pence. This is often confusing for investors used to seeing the usual dollars and cents convention.

Most U.K. stocks have a stamp duty of 50bps for buy transactions. Irish stocks have a stamp duty of 100bps for buy transactions. Irish stocks trading on the LSE still have a stamp duty of 100bps. Spain also applies a transfer tax.

Irish stocks trade on the LSE in EUR, not GBP.

Certain exchanges (Scandinavian primarily) do not support simple market orders electronically. Such orders must be entered with a limit. So an order to buy @ mkt is really entered as an order to buy with a limit @ best offer.

Many exchanges (Scandinavian and Swiss, for example) have tick increments. For example, if a stock in Sweden has tick increments of SEK 0.10, you cannot enter an order with an increment of SEK 0.07 without overriding the tick criteria on the exchange.

Germany has the shortest conventional settlement cycle in Europe, T+2 (trade date plus two business days). All other Western European cycles are T+3 (trade date plus three business days).

Most European markets have opening and closing auctions.

The German regional exchanges are some of the few remaining stock exchanges that still have physical floors.

PRACTICAL COMMENTARY CONCERNING TRADING, CLEARING, AND CUSTODY IN THE AMERICAS

TABLE 5.2 South American

Country	Exchanges	Central Securities Depository	Central Counterparty

Argentina	Bolsa de Cereales
	Bolsa de Comercio de
	  Buenos Aires
	Bolsa de Comercio de
	  Mar del Plata
	Bolsa de Comercio de
	  Rosario
	Bolsa de Comercio de
	  Santa Fe
	Mercado a Termino de
	  Rosario (ROFEX)
		Caja de Valores
		  (CVSA)
			Mercado de
			  Valores de
			  Buenos Aires
			  (MERVAL)

TABLE 5.2 (*Continued*)

Country	Exchanges	Central Securities Depository	Central Counterparty
Brazil	Bolsa de Mercadorias & Futuros (Brazilian Mercantile & Futures Exchange) Bolsa de Valores do Rio de Janeiro (Rio De Janeiro Stock Exchange) Bolsa do Brazil (Brazil Stock Exchange) (BOVESPA)	Companhia Brasileira de Liquidacao e Custodia (CBLC) Central de Custodia e Liquidacao Financeira de Titulos Privados (CETIP)	BM& FBOVESPA
Chile	Bolsa de Comercio de Santiago Bolsa Electronica de Chile	Deposito Central de Valores SA (DCV)	None
Colombia	Bolsa de Valores de Colombia (BVC)	Deposito Centralizado de Valores (DECEVAL)	None
Peru	Bolsa de Valores de Lima	CAVALI I.C.L.V. SA	CAVALI I.C.L.V. SA
Uruguay	Bolsa de Valores de Montevideo (BVM) Bolsa Electronica de Valores SA (BEVSA)	Bolsa de Valores de Montevideo (BVM)	None
Venezuela	Bolsa de Valores de Caracas (BVC)	Caja Venezolana de Valores (CVV)	None

Brazil is a registered market and requires CVM and BOVESPA identification/registration numbers to trade.

Argentina currency (peso) is not fully convertible and it is difficult to repatriate cap gains/commissions out of country.

TABLE 5.3   North America

Country	Exchanges	Central Securities Depository	Central Counterparty
Bermuda	Bermuda Stock Exchange (BSX)	Bermuda Securities Depository (BSD)	Bermuda Securities Depository (BSD)
Canada	Toronto Stock Exchange (TSX) Montreal Stock Exchange (MSE) Canadian Trading and Quotation System Inc. (CNQ)	Canadian Depository for Securities (CDS)	Canadian Depository for Securities (CDS)
Costa Rica	Bolsa Nacional de Valores de Costa Rica (BNV)	Central do Valores de la Bolsa Nacional de Valores SA (CEVAL)	None
Mexico	Mercado Mexicano de Derivados (Mex Der) Bolsa Mexicana de Valores (BMV)	S.D. INDEVAL SA de C.V. (INDEVAL)	Contreparte Central de Valores de Mexico SA
Puerto Rico	NYSE Euronext, AMEX, Nasdaq	Depository Trust Company (DTC)	National Securities Clearing Corporation
United States	NYSE Euronext, AMEX, Nasdaq	Depository Trust Company (DTC)	NSCC

PRACTICAL COMMENTARY CONCERNING TRADING, CLEARING, AND CUSTODY IN THE MIDDLE EAST AND AFRICA

TABLE 5.4 Middle East

Country	Exchanges	Central Securities Depository	Central Counterparty
Egypt	Egyptian Stock Exchange (EGX)	Misr for Clearing, Depository and Central Registry S.A.E. (MCDR)	None
Israel	Tel Aviv Stock Exchange (TASE)	Tel Aviv Stock Exchange (TASECH)	Tel Aviv Stock Exchange (TASECH)
Kazakhstan	Kazakhstan Stock Exchange (KASE)	Central Securities Depository (CJSC)	None
Morocco	Casablanca Stock Exchange (SBVC)	Maroclear	None
Turkey	Istanbul Stock Exchange (ISE)	Central Registry Agency (CRA)	None
UAE	Abu Dhabi Securities Market(ADX) Dubai Financial Market(DFM) Nasdaq Dubai	Central Securities Depository (CSD) as part of Nasdaq Dubai	Nasdaq Dubai

- Trading days in the Middle East are Sunday to Thursday.
- Bahrain—No single foreign individual can own more than 10 percent of a company.
- Qatar—Foreigners can own up to 25 percent of the shares of a company with some exceptions.
- Kuwait—Foreigners can only own up to 49 percent of banks, but no restrictions on other issuers of shares.
- UAE—Foreign ownership is restricted to 49 percent of an issuer's shares.
- All sales must be prevalidated in Middle Eastern markets (i.e., shares must be available for sale in the local broker's clearance account with the custodian before any sale). From a practical perspective, this means that active traders leave shares in the name of their local brokers whereas buy and hold investors will move shares to custody accounts ultimately held in their name at the CSD.

TABLE 5.5 Africa

Country	Exchanges	Central Securities Depository	Central Counterparty
Mauritius	Stock Exchange of Mauritius (SEM)	The Central Depository & Settlement Company Ltd.	The Central Depository & Settlement Company Ltd.
Namibia	Namibian Stock Exchange (NSX)	None	None
Nigeria	Nigeria Stock Exchange (NSE)	Central Securities Clearing System Limited (CSCS)	None
South Africa	Johannesburg Stock Exchange (JSE)	Strate Central Securities Depository (Strate)	None
Zambia	Lusaka Stock Exchange (LuSE)	Lusaka Stock Exchange Central Shares Depository (LCSD)	None
Zimbabwe	Zimbabwe Stock Exchange (ZSE)	None	None

PRACTICAL COMMENTARY CONCERNING TRADING, CLEARING, AND CUSTODY IN ASIA

TABLE 5.6 Asia

Country	Exchanges	Central Securities Depository	Central Counterparty
Australia	Australian Securities Exchange (ASX) Bendigo Stock Exchange (BSX) NSX National Stock Exchange of Australia	Austraclear, CHESS (The Clearing House Electronic Subregister System)	Australian Clearing House Limited (ACH)

TABLE 5.6 (*Continued*)

Country	Exchanges	Central Securities Depository	Central Counterparty
Bangladesh	Dhaka Stock Exchange (DSE) Chittagong Stock Exchange (CSE)	Central Depository Bangladesh Ltd. (CDBL)	None
China Shanghai	Shenzhen Stock Exchange Shanghai Stock Exchange	China Securities Depository and Clearing Corporation Ltd. (CSDCC)	China Securities Depository and Clearing Corporation Ltd. (CSDCC)
China Shenzen	Shenzhen Stock Exchange Shanghai Stock Exchange	China Securities Depository and Clearing Corporation Ltd. (CSDCC)	China Securities Depository and Clearing Corporation Ltd. (CSDCC)
Hong Kong	Stock Exchange of Hong Kong (SEHK)	Hong Kong Securities Clearing Company Limited (HKSCC)	Hong Kong Securities Clearing Company Limited (HKSCC)
Indonesia	Indonesia Stock Exchange (IdX)	Kustodian Sentral Efek Indonesia (KSEI)	Indonesian Clearing and Guarantee Co. (KPEI)
Japan	Fukuoka Stock Exchange JASDAQ Securities Exchange Nagoya Stock Exchange Osaka Securities Exchange Sapporo Securities Exchange Tokyo Stock Exchange	Japan Securities Depository Center (JASDEC)	JSCC, JDCC
Malaysia	Bursa Malaysia Kuala Lumpur Stock Exchange (KLSE)	Bursa Malaysia Depository Sdn. Bhd. (MCD)	None

(*Continued*)

TABLE 5.6 *(Continued)*

Country	Exchanges	Central Securities Depository	Central Counterparty
New Zealand	New Zealand Exchange Limited (NZX)	New Zealand Central Securities Depository Limited (NZCSD)	None
Pakistan	Karachi Stock Exchange (KSE) Lahore Stock Exchange (LSE) Islamabad Stock Exchange (ISE)	Central Depository Company of Pakistan Ltd. (CDC)	None
Philippines	Philippine Stock Exchange (PSE) Philippine Dealing & Exchange Corporation (PDEX)	Philippine Depository & Trust Corporation (PDTC)	Securities Clearing Corporation of the Philippines (SCCP)
Singapore	Singapore Exchange Limited (SGX)	The Central Depository (Pte) Limited (CDP), Singapore	The Central Depository (Pte) Limited (CDP), Singapore
South Korea	Korea Exchange (KRX)	Korea Securities Depository (KSD)	Korea Exchange (KRX)
Sri Lanka	Colombo Stock Exchange (CSE)	Central Depository System (Pvt) Limited (CDS)	None
Taiwan	Taiwan Stock Exchange (TWSE)	Taiwan Depository Clearing Corporation (TDCC)	Taiwan Stock Exchange (TWSE)
Thailand	Stock Exchange of Thailand (SET) Market for Alternative Investments (MAI) Thailand Futures Exchange (TFEX)	Thailand Securities Depository Ltd. (TSD)	Thailand Securities Depository Ltd. (TSD)

Many exchanges (Hong Kong, Japan, Taiwan, China) quote stocks with numbered tickers as opposed to lettered tickers.

Taiwan has the shortest settlement cycle, T+1, as well as the harshest penalty for failed trades: The account can be shut down for three years for failure to deliver shares.

Most stocks trade on exchange in board lots (i.e., 100 shares, 1,000 shares, based on price of stock). For orders that contain odd lots, many exchanges have set up odd lot boards in order to trade such components separately, often at a discount/premium to the main market.

The TSE (Tokyo Stock Exchange), Asia's biggest by market cap, still shuts down for an hour and a half for lunch break.

Taiwan, Malaysia, and Bangladesh are passenger markets, which require, among other things, the registration of the end investor with the local regulatory body. The broker-dealer must be given the registration number each time an order is entered into the market. Certain exemptions apply.

Some Asian markets do not have daylight saving time, so trading time of their markets varies relative to New York (i.e., sometimes Tokyo is 14 hours ahead of New York, while at other times it is only 13 hours ahead).

Australia, on the other hand, does have daylight saving time but because it is on the other side of the world from New York, at times Sydney is only 14 hours ahead, and other times it is as much as 16 hours ahead (when New York springs forward, Australia falls backward).

PASSENGER MARKETS

A passenger market is where the country's CSD requires that the securities be held in a segregated account in the name of the beneficial owner of the securities. This provides the government the ability to know who owns the country's securities, and helps identify who may not have been paying taxes or who might be accumulating a sizeable interest in a given issue.

There are three commonly recognized levels of beneficial ownership:

1. **Corporate.** Accounts opened under the corporate format would be for the benefit of the corporate entity, not any other underlying person or legal entity.
2. **Investment funds and trusts.** Accounts opened at this level would be for a legally recognized mutual fund, investment fund, or legal trust, each of which would have documentation of its status as a legal entity (for

example, a prospectus, offering letter, or documentation used to draw up the trust). These entities are not required to open accounts for each individual participant in the fund.

3. **Individuals.** Accounts under this level of ownership would be opened in the names of the individuals. These are investors who are investing outside of an investment fund. In many markets, joint accounts are not recognized. The account must be opened in the name or names of one or both of the beneficial owners, with the securities being allocated between the accounts.

Special note: For passenger market purposes, a registered representative or investment manager who has discretion over a securities account is not considered the account's beneficial owner. By way of example, if a registered representative has 10 clients who want to trade in a passenger market, the registered representative must open 10 accounts.[1] Discretion over a securities account does not equate to beneficial ownership.

The operational problem with passenger markets is that individual accounts must be set up and operated by the subcustodian and CSD, and also at the investor's brokerage firm (or clearing broker). This is inefficient and is one of the factors that raises the cost of global investing.[2]

CASE STUDY RELATING TO PASSENGER MARKETS

The following case study illustrates potential traps for unwary investors who trade in passenger markets.

The Bangladesh Matter

In 2007, eight clients of a U.S. broker trading in Bangladesh began accumulating shares of ABC Ltd. (ABC Bank), a Bangladeshi company that trades on the Bangladesh exchange. Ultimately, the investors accumulated 694,860

---

[1]Note that some passenger markets, such as Korea, offer alternative holding arrangements under which brokers and custodians may open nominee-type accounts in the broker's or custodian's name. They will be required to disclose the names of the customers on request from the regulators.

[2]Incredible as it may sound, there are more than 80 million individual accounts at the Chinese depository.

shares. The combined holdings exceeded 5 percent of the outstanding shares, although no single investor's holdings exceeded that amount. Pursuant to Bangladeshi securities laws, the accumulation of more than 5 percent of a company's shares by a single shareholder triggered a three-year holding period for the shares. Attempts by the broker's clients to sell their ABC Bank shares were initially blocked by the Bangladeshi exchange because, on the depository record, it looked as if the broker (through its subcustodian) beneficially owned the shares. The shares were later unrestricted from sale, but this matter is illustrative of the care that must be taken with passenger markets.

CHAPTER 6

Legal Framework of the World Markets

Much of our U.S. and EU legal traditions have been exported to or adopted in the global securities markets, so a high-level understanding of U.S. laws and EU Directives is desirable. Before delving into more specifics of securities regulation in the United States and EU, it is worth pausing to reflect on why governments regulate the capital markets at all.

It has long been recognized that the free flow of capital and credit creates a multiplier effect on a nation's economy, so governments recognize that it is important that financial services firms do not fail. Moreover, the major financial services players—banks, insurance companies, pension funds, investment funds—all have one thing in common, namely, that they take in deposits (or premiums or contributions in the case of insurance companies and pension funds, respectively) not knowing with certainty when they will have to pay funds out. Consequently, financial services firms are highly regulated for two purposes. First, regulation is for the good of the economy so that credit can flow freely, and second, so that financial services firms do not fail and harm their depositors or pensioners or investors. It is this dual purpose that makes financial services regulation unique.[1]

---

[1]The existence of government-sponsored insurance protection programs for the customers of banks and securities firms (such as FDIC and SIPC insurance in the United States) is another justification for governmental regulation. SIPC and other protection programs are discussed in Chapter 15.

A BRIEF HISTORY OF U.S. REGULATION

Only history can explain the patchwork of state and federal agencies involved in regulating banks, securities, and insurance in the United States.

By the time Franklin Delano Roosevelt took office on March 4, 1933, more than 10,000 of the approximately 25,000 banks that had been in existence in 1929 had disappeared. A rash of bank failures in 1932 and 1933 led Congress to act. Moreover, the investigations of a hard-charging former prosecutor, Ferdinand Pecora, caused the public to place the blame for bank failures on securities speculation by banks. The truth appears to be that there was little real evidence of bank-affiliated securities firms involved in financial misdealings. Nonetheless, the evidence brought forward by Pecora of wrongdoing by large New York banks led Congress to clip the wings of those primarily big banks that engaged in commercial and investment banking together. The public was outraged and Main Street wanted revenge on Wall Street for the Great Depression.[2]

Equally as significant as the separation of commercial and investment banking by the National Banking Act of 1933 (commonly known as Glass-Steagall after its legislative sponsors) was the creation by Glass-Steagall of federal deposit insurance. Proponents of federal deposit insurance successfully argued that it should not be used to prop up, indirectly, speculative investments made by securities affiliates of federally insured banks. Thus was born the separation of commercial and investment banking that existed for more than half of the twentieth century in the United States.

THE NEW DEAL AND GLASS-STEAGALL

The Banking Act of 1933 was not legislation in a vacuum; it was an integral part of revolutionary New Deal reform legislation. Although many states had earlier passed so-called *blue sky* laws to prevent fraud in connection

---

[2]For a recent history of the events leading up to the Great Depression and the men who contributed to it read, Liaquat Ahamed, *The Lords of Finance—The Bankers Who Broke the World* (Penguin Press 2009). Not unlike Newton in the South Sea Bubble, the greatest economist of the age, John Maynard Keynes, lost considerable sums trading his own account in the 1929 stock market crash.

with the sale of securities (so named because it was said that unscrupulous brokers would sell unsuspecting investors stock in so many feet of clear blue sky), the Congressional passage of the Securities Act of 1933 and its sister act, the Securities Exchange Act of 1934 (which created the SEC), did more than anything else to rid the securities business of fraud and manipulation. Although similar federal reform of the insurance industry was also contemplated, insurance regulation was decisively left to the states when Congress passed the McCarran-Ferguson Act of 1945. With federal legislation governing mutual funds companies and investment advisers, as well as thrifts and credit unions, all passed by 1940, the legal framework governing the financial services industry in the United States was largely in place for post–World War II expansion.

By the late 1980s, holes appeared in the patchwork quilt of financial regulation. The Federal Reserve Board took the lead in narrowing the reach of Glass-Steagall. A closely followed example of this was a board ruling that an affiliate of a bank could engage in the private placement of commercial paper. The decision was challenged by a securities industry trade group, but it was upheld.

The camel's nose was in the tent. Subsequently, the Federal Reserve Board ruled that a bank affiliate could be in the securities business as long as it derived no more than 10 percent of its revenues from underwriting or dealing in securities that the bank could not otherwise underwrite or trade. Thus, banks that were government securities dealers and had large revenues from that eligible form of securities activity for banks were able to back-door their way into underwriting and selling corporate stocks and bonds.

The fact that large banks already owned securities affiliates by the time the Gramm-Leach-Bliley Act in 1999 officially repealed Glass-Steagall may have diminished the significance of the repeal to the general public.[3]

After the financial panic of 2008, some called for the reinstatement of Glass-Steagall, but many felt the United States would be uncompetitive in the global marketplace should this happen. The Dodd-Frank Wall Street Reform and Consumer Protection Act enacted in 2010 left the essential U.S. regulatory infrastructure in place with greater authority for the Federal Reserve Board and seemingly more coordination of regulatory bodies

---

[3]Saudi Arabia recently took a different approach by deciding to separate the regulation of banking firms and securities firms from what had earlier been consolidated regulation.

through a Financial Stability Oversight Council and more information gathering through the Office of Financial Research. The legislation did not turn back the clock and reestablish Glass-Steagall. However, important reforms were implemented, namely, higher capital requirements for banks (along with stricter leverage and liquidity requirements—all to be coordinated with international standards); limits on perceived risky proprietary trading, and the creation of a central clearing counterparty for certain derivatives. One of the most significant, but least discussed reforms, was the creation of a new orderly liquidation regime for systemically important financial institutions that trumps traditional insolvency regimes for smaller banks, insurance companies, and broker-dealers.

Unlike the patchwork of regulators in the United States, other countries (notably the United Kingdom, Germany, and Singapore) have consolidated supervision in one regulator.[4] Seemingly more efficient, a debate rages over whether a monolithic form of regulator imperils the regulator's effectiveness because (1) a "one size fits all" regulator may get spread too thin and lose the in-depth specialization of narrowly focused regulators, or (2) a monopolistic regulator may grow overly complacent in its role if not constantly challenged by sister regulators.[5] The International Organization of Securities Commissions (IOSCO) acts as a coordinating body internationally for securities regulators worldwide and can fill a role in stimulating securities law reform. Much information on international initiatives may be obtained on its website at www.iosco.org.[6] More broadly, the Financial Stability Board serves a similar function as a clearinghouse for ideas about how nations should regulate financial services firms, particularly banks. This board, previously known as the Financial Stability Forum, was itself an outgrowth of the failure of a European bank in the mid-1970s that posed systemic risk to the European banking system. The Financial Stability Board is housed

---

[4]With a change in government in 2010, new leaders announced plans to abolish the single regulator in the United Kingdom in its current form. Instead, the new government proposed that a Financial Policy Committee be established within the Bank of England and be responsible for macro-prudential regulation. Prudential regulation of banks, building societies, insurers, and dealers would pass to another agency within the Bank of England and consumer protection to yet a third body.

[5]Philip R. Wood, *International Loans, Bonds and Securities Regulation* (Sweet & Maxwell 1995).

[6]The Council of European Regulators (CESR) fulfills the function for Europe and the North American Securities Administrators Association serves the role for the states in the United States.

within the Bank of International Settlements (BIS) in Basel, Switzerland. The BIS, the bank to central banks formed after World War I, is perhaps best known for developing the international guidelines for capital requirements for banks.[7] In light of the bank bailouts in 2008 and 2009, the BIS has been the subject of much criticism and has subsequently revised and enhanced international banking capital standards.

THE PANIC OF 2008 IN CONTEXT

When former Chairman of the Federal Reserve Alan Greenspan testified to Congress in October 2008 that the intellectual edifice had collapsed in the summer of 2007, he was talking about the entire regulatory framework and risk management system underpinning the U.S. financial services industry. To be sure, immediate causes of the 2008 panic are readily apparent. To name four:

1. The Taxpayer Relief Act of 1997 eliminating capital gains taxes on primary residences and thereby precipitating a housing boom aided and abetted by a government policy encouraging home ownership whether through the operations of quasi-governmental agencies such as Fannie Mae and Freddie Mac or through bank community reinvestment mandates.
2. The failure of the Commodity Futures Modernization Act of 2000 to comprehensively regulate derivatives.
3. The development of a securitized debt market where the persons having direct contact with the borrower obtained origination fees but did not assume any credit risk on the loan and where investors who bought these securitized loans overly relied on rating agencies to assess their risk.
4. An excessive use of leverage underpinned by faulty risk metrics and lax credit extension policies.

---

[7]In theory, the Bank of International Settlements and the League of Nations would have brought international peace and financial stability to the globe after World War I. In a triumph of hope over experience, the United Nations and the International Monetary Fund were created after World War II for the same purpose.

Focusing on these immediate causes, however, is like focusing on the political rivalries in the Balkans as the cause of World War I. The real cause was much more fundamental in that there had been a philosophical shift in the role of regulation and government enforcement in relation to financial services.

To Tres Arnett
With best wishes,
Ronald Reagan

When Ronald Reagan was elected president of the United States in 1980, he heralded a restored faith in the power of the market to be self-policing rather than a need for government to police the markets. This vision quickly permeated the Western world and government regulation waned during a period of unprecedented economic expansion. Was it an absence of the right laws and regulations that led to the 2008 recession? The answer is clearly no, in most cases. As an example, even advocates of a new Consumer Financial Protection Agency in the United States have acknowledged that the laws were on the books to prevent misleading information from being disseminated by banks and brokers in connection with home mortgages. As a result of the deregulatory trend, some surmise, there was no will to enforce those laws.

In the assessment of the Bank for International Settlements, the Panic of 2008 is attributable, in part, to senior managers and boards of directors who were not asking the right questions or listening to the right people. With hindsight in respect to some institutions, this is an accurate conclusion. However, a more interesting question is whether the panic was part of a larger business cycle or broader macroeconomic trend, even beyond the global imbalance of payments between the Western world and the oil-producing states and China.

Consider the chart in Figure 6.1, modeled after the famous Russian economist Nikolai Kondratieff. In context, the 2008 credit crisis looks like a small event amid much larger expansions and contractions. Nonetheless, because the legal framework and regulatory scheme govern how we must act today, they remain important in the quotidian functioning of investors

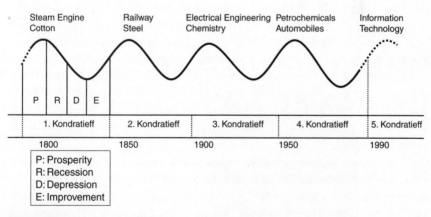

FIGURE 6.1 The Kondratieff Chart

U.S. Supreme Court. This court has defined "securities," "fraud," and "stock manipulation."

and those who support investors. Therefore, the next few pages explore in greater depth specific U.S. laws and EU Directives.

THE PILLARS OF U.S. FEDERAL SECURITIES LAW

There were six pillars of securities reform enacted during the wake of the Great Depression. Four are still actively in play in today's brokerage community—the Securities Act of 1933 (the 1933 Act, governing the new issue of securities), the Securities Exchange Act of 1934 (the 1934 Act, governing securities exchanges, the licensing of brokers, periodic reporting by issuers and other miscellaneous securities market concerns), the Investment Advisers Act of 1940 (the Advisers Act, governing those who provide investment advice for a fee), and the Investment Company Act of 1940 (the 1940 Act, governing investment funds, primarily those sold to the public such as mutual funds). Each of these laws will be examined below.

The remaining two acts deserve brief mention for completeness. Somewhat less well known, but still perhaps one of the most important of the six major securities laws passed in the United States at the end of the Great Depression, is the Trust Indenture Act of 1939. This act governs the functions of the custodial banks that perform the role of paying agents and trustees in connection with corporate and government debt. The remaining act was the Public Utility Holding Company Act.[8]

The following is a brief summary of the principal features of the acts relevant today to the brokerage community.[9]

Securities Act of 1933

This Act applies primarily to the initial offering of securities by issuers as opposed to secondary market trading. The SEC has stated that the 1933 Act has two basic objectives: (1) to require that investors receive financial and other significant information concerning securities being offered for public sale; and (2) to prohibit deceit, misrepresentations, and other fraud in the sale of securities. A primary means of accomplishing these goals is to require the disclosure of important financial information by issuers of securities through the registration of those securities with the SEC. This information enables investors, rather than regulators, to make informed judgments about whether to purchase a company's securities. This is the most philosophically important piece of the legislation, namely that investors should decide what good investments are—not regulators. Although the SEC requires that the information be accurate, it does not guarantee it. Investors who purchase securities and suffer losses have important recovery rights against issuers of securities if they can prove that there was incomplete or inaccurate disclosure of important information.

In general, securities sold in the United States by U.S. or foreign issuers must be registered with the SEC unless they are offered in private placements. The registration process and associated disclosure materials (such as the

---

[8]The final seminal piece of Great Depression securities legislation was the Public Utility Holding Company Act. It is a historic anomaly born of the need to regulate power suppliers whose activities surged with the growth of radio, electric lighting, and modern kitchen appliances in the 1920s. This Act also sought to prevent the financial chicanery that had occurred when Samuel Insull, a public utility holding company executive, misled investors by using an array of opaque subsidiaries.

[9]The summaries are drawn, in part, from the SEC's descriptions of the statutes it enforces. More information can be found at www.sec.gov.

prospectus) provide essential facts about the issuer. In general, issuers must provide:

- A description of the issuer's properties and business
- A description of the security to be offered for sale
- Information about the management of the issuer
- Financial statements certified by independent accountants

The information must be contained in prospectuses delivered to investors at the time of the sale of the securities. These statements and the accompanying prospectuses become public shortly after filing, and investors can access them using the SEC's EDGAR database.

Not all offerings of securities must be registered with the SEC. Some exemptions from the registration requirement include:

- Private offerings to a limited number of persons or institutions
- Offerings of limited size
- Offerings occurring entirely within a single state
- Securities of municipal, state, and federal governments

The SEC has stated that by exempting many small offerings from the registration process, it seeks to foster capital formation by lowering the cost of offering securities to the public. These registration exemptions generally do not mandate the delivery of the same level of information as is required for registered offerings. However, issuers most often do deliver similar information in response to regulatory actions and federal and state judicial decisions imposing disclosure obligations on issuers. The SEC's Division of Corporate Finance has first-line responsibility for administering the 1933 Act.

Securities Exchange Act of 1934

The 1934 Act largely targets the securities markets and their participants. With this Act, Congress created the SEC. The 1934 Act empowers the SEC with broad authority over all aspects of the securities industry, including the power to register, regulate, and oversee brokerage firms, transfer agents, and clearing agencies as well as securities self-regulatory organizations (SROs) such as the Financial Institutions Regulatory Authority (known as FINRA).[10]

The 1934 Act also identifies and prohibits market manipulation and other types of fraudulent conduct in the markets and provides the SEC with disciplinary powers over broker-dealers and other regulated entities and individuals associated with them. The Act also empowers the SEC to require periodic reporting of information by companies with publicly traded securities.

Companies with more than $10 million in assets whose securities are held by more than 500 owners must file annual and other periodic reports, regardless of whether their securities have been offered publicly. These reports are available to the public through the SEC's EDGAR database.

The 1934 Act also governs proxy statements used by public companies for annual or special shareholder meetings and requires disclosure of important information by anyone seeking to acquire more than 5 percent of a public company's securities by direct purchase or tender offer. This allows shareholders to make informed decisions on these critical corporate events.

The Act requires a variety of market participants to register with the SEC, including exchanges, brokers and dealers, transfer agents, and clearing agencies; such registration involves filing disclosure documents that are updated on a regular basis.

The exchanges and FINRA are identified as SROs. SROs must create rules that allow for disciplining members due to improper conduct, and for establishing measures to ensure market integrity and investor protection. SRO-proposed rules are published for comment before final SEC review and approval. The SEC's Division of Market Regulation has responsibility for administering many of the provisions of the 1934 Act.

Before examining the remaining two important statutes passed in 1940, measures to prevent stock manipulation are addressed.

---

[10] FINRA is a relatively unique body in the world of securities regulation enforcement. A private body, FINRA is funded by the brokerage community to police itself. FINRA's work is overseen by the SEC.

Stock Manipulation

In English common law, market manipulation has been a violation of law since the 1800s; see *Scott v. Brown*, 1892, 2 Q.B. 724, 61 L.J. (N.S.). Following the fabled "pool operations" of the 1920s,[11] the United

The Classic Way to Manipulate a Stock Was to "Paint the Tape." A painted tape was a series of fictitious trades that would be posted to the ticker tape and might show advancing prices or increased volumes (suggesting investor demand for the stock). An unsuspecting investor might buy or sell based on the false information he read on the tape.

---

[11] For an entertaining description of the colorful figures of the 1920s and 1930s, see John Brooks, *Once in Golconda* (Norton 1969). For a good articulation of the elements of stock

States, through the 1934 Act, sought to statutorily outlaw stock manipulation. Pool operations, like the stock manipulations of today, had many of the same features. Joseph Kennedy, the father of the great president John F. Kennedy, was a well-known participant in pool operations in the 1920s.[12]

Pool operations worked like this. A conspiracy of investors would obtain control of the issued and outstanding shares of a company (the float). Through false rumors or trades in which prices were seemingly raised by matched trades or wash sales (in which beneficial ownership did not really change), the unsuspecting public would be induced into buying shares. The operators would then unload their stocks for a profit. In 1934, outlawing stock manipulation was seen as the centerpiece of the 1934 Act (specifically, prohibiting matched trades, wash sales, and other deceptive trading practices, which could create an appearance of rising stock prices when, in fact, there was no such thing).[13]

In time, judges, using the elasticity of the common law, implied to a private person the right to sue for fraud under the 1934 Act.[14] Thus, the 1934 Act became the principal means by which regulators could deter fraud and market abuse, and private investors could recover damages from those who engaged in financial chicanery.

---

manipulation in the United States, see *Crane Co. v. Westinghouse Air Brake Co.*, 419 F.2d 787 (2d Cir. 1969). At a practical level, compliance officers watch for movements of large blocks of (typically, low-priced) stock seemingly without economic justification or at rapidly increasing prices coupled with Internet chat room rumors. These are hallmarks of a stock manipulation.

[12] President Roosevelt, specifically because of Kennedy's knowledge and expertise in the securities markets, appointed him the first head of the SEC. To some, it seemed Roosevelt was setting a wolf to guard the sheep.

[13] One of the most colorful of all stock manipulations was that perpetrated by the confederates of Lord Cochrane, an acclaimed British Naval officer, on the eve of the defeat of Napoleon at the Battle of Waterloo. A conspirator falsely posted news to the English Admiralty of Napoleon's defeat and rode into London with the false news. Cochrane and others profited handsomely, having bought a popular stock whose price soared on the news. The conspirators were prosecuted criminally under the theory that the false news distorted the interest rate the English government had to offer to raise funds. Whether Cochrane was truly guilty is a matter of debate. As a great British naval officer ostracized from his home country, Cochrane later assisted in the liberation of a number of Latin American countries from Spain. See Robert Harvey, *Cochrane: The Life and Exploits of a Fighting Captain* (Da Capo Press 2001). Cochrane's exploits are, in part, the basis for Patrick O'Brien's "Master and Commander" novels.

[14] *Blue Chip Stamps v. Manor Drug Stores*, 421 U.S. 723 (1975).

Investment Company Act of 1940

The 1940 Act regulates the formation and operation of investment companies, including mutual funds, that engage primarily in investing, reinvesting, and trading in securities, and whose own securities are offered to the investing public. The Act is designed to minimize conflicts of interest that arise in the complex operations of investment funds. The focus of the 1940 Act is on disclosure to the investing public of information about the fund and its investment objectives, as well as on investment company structure and operations. It is important to remember that the 1940 Act does not permit the SEC to supervise directly the investment decisions or activities of these companies or to judge the merits of their investments. The Act also indirectly sets standards for private funds such as hedge funds by establishing exemptions that limit the number and/or qualifications of investors in such funds. The SEC's Division of Investment Management has first-line responsibility for administering the 1940 Act.

Investment Advisers Act of 1940

The Advisers Act generally requires that persons compensated for advising others about securities investments must register with the SEC and conform to regulations designed to protect investors. In the past advisers who had 15 or more clients and who had at least $25 million of assets under management were required to register with the SEC. The Dodd-Frank financial reforms amended the Advisers Act so that effective July 2011 each adviser with a place of business in the United States must register either with the SEC or with the state authorities in the state in which the adviser maintains its principal office. Advisers with $100 million or more of assets under management are required to register only with the SEC. Also, advisers that advise one or more SEC-registered investment companies or that market their advisory services to the public in the United States must register with the SEC or in some cases with the state authorities. Advisers based outside of the United States need only register with the SEC if they have 15 or more U.S. clients or investors in funds managed by advisers. These changes will force most U.S.-based hedge fund and private equity fund managers with $150 million or more of assets under management to register with the SEC and provide regular financial reports to the federal regulators. These changes were made in order to shine more light into the often opaque world of private money management. The SEC's Division of Investment Management has first-line responsibility for administering the Advisers Act.

Suffice it to say, the sea change brought about by the U.S. federal securities laws enacted after the Great Depression was to turn the sale of securities from "buyer beware" (caveat emptor) to "seller beware" (caveat vendor). The hallmark of the 1933 Act was the requirement that issuers of securities make meaningful disclosures about their companies so that the public could be informed and choose freely whether to invest in a new offering of securities based on accurate information. Unlike prior attempts at regulation (most notably the blue-sky laws passed by the various states that make up the United States), the federal regime would not step in to prevent sales of securities as long as there was robust disclosure and the absence of fraud.[15] Disclosure was and is the heart of the 1933 Act and disclosure is also the theme underlying the periodic financial reporting requirements of the 1934 Act. Under the 1934 Act, exchange-traded companies must report periodically their financials in a specified format to the SEC. This financial reporting is made available to investors for their evaluation through mandated disclosure imposed on issuers of securities.[16]

---

[15] As Supreme Court Justice Louis Brandeis has said, "Sunlight is said to be the best of disinfectants; electric light the most efficient policeman." It is this thinking that underpins the entire emphasis on disclosure to investors of accurate facts about a company. The counterbalance, in the event of improper disclosure, is the investor's ability to sue for fraud. Fraud, like the definition of a security, can sometimes escape definition. In fact, there is no federal statutory definition of fraud in the United States. It is remarkable that "securities" and "fraud" can have such undefined edges. Notwithstanding this observation, a person is liable for securities fraud when he, with knowledge, makes a materially false statement (or fails to say something when he should have) in connection with the purchase or sale of a security, on which another person justifiably relied to his detriment. *Basic v. Levinson*, 485 U.S. 224 (1988); *Derry v. Peek*, 14 App. Cas. 337 (1889). "Knowing" something can also be a bit elastic. In the law, turning a "blind eye" to something—not wanting to know something—can be the equivalent of knowledge. The British call this *Nelsonian blindness* after Lord Horatio Nelson. The famous British naval hero reputedly put a telescope to his patched eye and famously declared he did not see his commander's signal to retreat from the French at the Battle of the Nile. Nelson did not want to see his commander's signal because he wanted to attack the French and win a great battle. Nelson, flamboyantly ignoring the signal, attacked and won the battle. Thus was born the term *Nelsonian blindness*.
[16] The details of the SEC disclosure regime are set forth, among other places, in Charles J. Johnson Jr. and Joseph McLaughlin, *Corporate Finance and the Securities Law* (Aspen Publishers 2004).

A RECENT HISTORY OF EUROPEAN LEGISLATION

Just as U.S. federal legislation transcended the law of the states that make up the United States it is interesting to note that the recent European effort to harmonize securities law through EU Directives (implemented by the EU member states pursuant to country-specific legislation) is a comparable effort.

In 1999, the EU adopted the Financial Services Action Plan (FSAP) to set the framework for the development of the European Securities Market in the twenty-first century. The objectives of the FSAP were:

- A single market in the EU for wholesale financial services
- Open and secure retail financial services markets in the EU
- State-of-the-art prudential rules and supervision in the EU

The FSAP originally comprised 42 measures, the majority of which were adopted by 2005.

Although some of the inspiration for EU securities law has come from various national laws, it is a distinctive body of law that represents important steps toward a supranational body of EU securities law. The eight most important directives are described next.

The Hungarian Parliament, pictured above, is responsible for passing national laws to implement EU Directives in Hungary.

MiFID

The Markets in Financial Instruments Directive, or MiFID, is commonly used to refer not only to the Markets in Financial Instruments Directive (Directive 2004/39/EC) adopted by the EU in 2004, but also to a supplemental EU Regulation and Directive, which came fully into effect on November 1, 2007. The initial thrust of MiFID was to build on the Investment Services Directive of 1993 (Directive 93/22/EC), which established a "passporting regime" such that investment firms authorized in one EU member state could, subject to applying for a passport, provide services or establish a branch to provide services in another EU member state. MiFID not only simplified this regime through making authorization in one member state effectively equal to authorization across the whole EU, but also established a common set of rules across a range of areas, notably that of conduct, generally. Thus, MiFID and its associated Directive and Regulation set common rules for best execution, transaction reporting, outsourcing, relations with customers (including assessment of suitability and appropriateness, and conduct in portfolio management and contracting with customers), and treatment of customer assets and monies.

The bulk of the rules made under MiFID are given effect into the national legislation of each of the EU member states. In practice, the level of detail in MiFID means that national rules in the areas covered by MiFID are now substantively in line. In addition, the Committee of European Securities Regulators (CESR) has issued guidance on a number of MiFID rules to ensure common interpretations across the EU.

The Settlement Finality Directive

The Settlement Finality Directive (SFD; Directive 98/26/EC as amended by Directive 2009/44/EC) is another measure born out of FSAP and is aimed at reducing the systemic risk associated with participation in payment and securities settlement systems and, in particular, the risk linked to the insolvency of a participant in such a system. It applies to payment and securities settlement systems as well as any participant in such a system, and to collateral security provided in connection with the participation in a system or operations of the central banks in the member states of the EU in their functions as central banks.

The SFD provides that transfer orders entered into systems cannot be revoked or invalidated by stipulating the irrevocability and finality of transfer orders and of the netting of transfers, even if a system participant is subject to insolvency proceedings. It is important to note that this applies only once the settlement has occurred in the system, so that, for example, in the recent Lehman Brothers insolvency, trades that were matched in Euroclear (Euroclear Bank SA) could be unmatched by one of the counterparties as long as they have not actually gone through the overnight processing in Euroclear and settled. The SFD, in other words, prevents the unwinding of completed settlements. It does not address trades that are just in the process of settlement where it can still be stopped by the participant under the settlement system's own rules.

The recent amendment of the SFD extends the protection of the SFD to nighttime settlement and settlements between interoperable systems (i.e., settlement systems that have allowed other settlement systems to access each other in line with EU requirements so as to increase competition in this area and operate cross-border).

Financial Collateral Directive

The Financial Collateral Arrangements Directive (FCD; Directive 2002/47/EC as amended by Directive 2009/44/EC) aims to create a harmonized EU framework that improves enforceability and limits credit risk in relation to cross-border financial collateral arrangements, including in the event of insolvency of the party providing collateral, whether the collateral is provided in the form of cash or securities. The arrangements must be evidenced in writing or other enforceable legal manner. The FCD applies both where collateral is taken by transferring the title with the intention of returning equivalent collateral when the secured obligation is discharged and to collateral taken by a security interest over the collateral is created and the collateral is under the control of the collateral taker. The amendment of the FCD extended the scope to include credit claims in order to facilitate their use throughout the EU.

The Market Abuse Directive

The Directive on Insider Dealing and Market Manipulation (Directive 2003/6/EC), otherwise known as "The Market Abuse Directive," sets out a regime in respect of certain types of market conduct, in particular, where these may cause market mechanisms to cease to operate effectively either by (a) distorting supply or demand for one or more instruments or the price for which they are purchased or sold, or (b) creating a false impression as to the supply or price of an instrument or as to the intended or actual conduct of one or more players in the market.

In addition, the Directive outlines a range of preventive measures that companies are required to adopt in order to combat insider dealing. Such measures include the maintenance of "insider lists" of people who have access to inside information, the disclosure and control of such inside information, the disclosure of dealings in the company's securities, and the reporting of suspicious transactions.

In many ways, the Directive builds on established principles of criminal law and tort law (notably, deceit), and represents an important step at the EU level in establishing conduct that may be punished, including by criminal sanctions. Prior to the Directive's implementation, member states had different powers, approaches, and systems for tackling market abuse and manipulation. The Directive introduced an EU-wide market abuse regime and established a framework for facilitating the proper flow of information to the market. It was designed to improve confidence in the integrity of the integrated EU market and foster greater cross-border cooperation (which was particularly important given the increasing volumes of cross-border trading).

The Prospectus Directive

The Prospectus Directive (Directive 2003/71/EC) sets forth the overarching scheme surrounding the disclosure requirement for the new issue of securities. EU member states will not allow offers of securities to be made to the public without the prior publication of an approved prospectus. However, once approved in one member state, the prospectus can be used to market securities across all EU member states, thus acting as a single "passport" for issuers once approved. In order to ensure investor protection, that approval is granted only if the prospectus meets common EU standards for what information must be disclosed and how.

The Transparency Directive

The Transparency Directive (Directive 2004/109/EC) is a directive on the harmonization of transparency requirements for information about issuers whose securities are admitted to trading on a regulated market in the EU. It establishes minimum requirements on periodic financial reporting and on the disclosure of major shareholdings for issuers whose securities are admitted to trading on a regulated market. The Transparency Directive also deals with how this information should be stored and disseminated. The key aim of the Directive is to improve the efficiency, openness, and integrity of the EU capital markets, thereby enhancing investor protection and attracting investors to the EU marketplace.

The Capital Requirements Directive

The Capital Requirements Directive (CRD; Directive 2006/48/EC and Directive 2006/49/EC) stipulates minimum capital requirements that banks and investment firms are required to meet to ensure that they maintain sufficient levels of capital reserves relative to their risk exposure. The Directive aims to create a framework within the EU that is consistent with the international framework for capital requirements (Basel II) adopted by the Basel Committee on Banking Supervision.

In October 2008, the Commission announced its proposals to revise the current rules, with the objectives of reinforcing the stability of the financial system, reducing risk exposure and improving the supervision of banks that operate in more than one EU member state. A directive amending the CRD and implementing these new proposals was adopted by the Commission in May 2009. The amendments to the CRD are aimed at improving transparency, supervision, and risk management in the financial section to avoid future repetition of the current financial crisis. Further amendments are proposed in relation to capital requirements for re-securitizations held in trading books, disclosures about securitization risks, and compensation policies for banks and investment firms.

The Alternative Investment Fund Managers Directive

The Alternative Investment Fund Managers Directive (the AIFM Directive) calls for greater regulation, on a pan-European basis, of investment funds and, in particular, private equity and hedge funds. It also has important implications for custodians of securities based in the EU. The AIFM Directive introduces a regulatory framework for managers of any collective investment undertaking if the investment manager is domiciled in the EU, or if the fund is domiciled or marketed within the EU, and the manager has assets under management in excess of €100 million. Although the political focus has primarily been on private equity and hedge funds, the AIFM Directive extends to all types of collective investment undertaking, other than those that fall within the remit of the UCITS Directive (Directive 85/611/EEC), and, as such, includes hedge funds, funds of hedge funds, private equity funds, real estate funds, infrastructure funds, and long-only funds.

The Directive imposes a number of requirements on alternative investment fund managers (AIFMs) that fall within its scope, including requirements relating to the separation of portfolio management and risk management, restrictions on delegation, prefiling of fund documentation, minimum capital requirements, ongoing disclosure to investors and regulators, and other additional compliance obligations. AIFMs will also be required to appoint a sole depositary to act as custodian for each fund and also to have responsibility for monitoring of the fund's operation and cash flows, imposing limits on leverage and arranging independent valuations. For its part, the custodian is responsible on essentially a strict liability basis for any assets placed with the custodian but later found to be missing.

A couple of the most controversial features of the AIFM Directive calls for money managers to implement remuneration policies for all relevant staff including adding deferral of remuneration in order to incent better long-term risk management and clawbacks of payments from employees in the case of malfeasance by them and, in a measure described by many as being protectionist, the requirement for funds and managers from third countries, that is, non-EU countries, to comply with certain aspects of the Directive in order to market to EU investors. Practically, it is envisioned that a passporting regime will be established, namely a mechanism will be set up whereby if firms meet certain standards, they will be allowed to market in all EU countries.

Member states are likely to be required to implement the provisions of the Directive by the end of 2012 or early 2013.

The New European Super-Regulators

In September 2009, the European Commission published its proposals to change the current regulatory and supervisory framework in Europe with the creation of the European Systemic Risk Board (ESRB), which will undertake macro-prudential supervision. Its role will include the detection of risks to the financial system and provide recommendations for action. Under the proposed new framework, three new European Supervisory Authorities (ESAs) will be established to oversee the regulation of the banking, insurance, and occupational pensions and securities sectors, namely the European Banking Authority (EBA), the European Insurance and Occupational Pensions Authority (EIOPA), and the European Securities and Markets Authority (ESMA).

The creation of the ESAs signals what many commentators regard as a progressive shift of power away from national regulation toward a more centralized system of regulation with the ESAs to be granted wide powers to formulate policy, monitor national supervisors' implementation of EU regulations, impose supervisory decisions on financial institutions, impose prohibitions or restrictions on certain activities, and, in certain exceptional circumstances, to overrule national supervisors. The new regulatory framework is expected to be in place by early 2011.

A BRIEF COMPARISON OF U.S. LAWS AND EU DIRECTIVES

Many of the important EU Directives have direct analogues to the U.S. laws and regulations. In the Prospectus Directive one can see the disclosure requirements of the 1933 Act. In the Transparency Directive are the periodic reporting requirements of the 1934 Act. The Market Abuse Directive encompasses the insider trading and fraud provisions of the 1934 Act. Other Directives not specifically mentioned above, like the Capital Risk Directive, find their analogue in the Net Capital Rule (77 U.S.C. § 15c3-1). A major

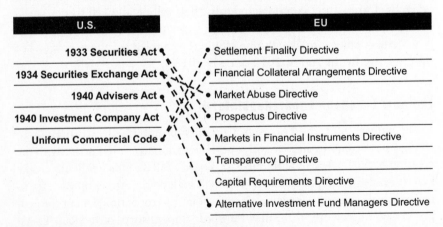

FIGURE 6.2   Significant European and U.S. Laws.

piece of legislation, the Take Over Directive, which demands that shareholders of a corporation holding more than an established percentage of shares (for example, 30 percent) must acquire the remaining shares at a fair price, has no analogue in U.S. federal law, although there are some equivalents under state law. In the United States, minority shareholders are left to sue in state courts if they are oppressed by controlling shareholders. Figure 6.2 lists important U.S. laws and EU Directives and visually connects the analogous provisions. Happily, from an investor protection perspective, the same themes are covered in each jurisdiction.

CHAPTER 7

Transfer of Securities and Perfection of Collateral

Just as the 1933, 1934, 1939, and two 1940 Acts reshaped the U.S. securities markets by delivering a comprehensive legal framework,[1] model uniform laws developed by the Uniform Law Commissioners and implemented voluntarily by each of the 50 states delivered one legal structure for the transfer of securities (Article 8 of the Uniform Commercial Code) and one set of uniform rules for perfecting legal claims to collateral (Article 9 of the Uniform Commercial Code). When coupled with the Federal Bankruptcy Code and the Federal Securities Insurance Protection Act (SIPA), the governing body of law surrounding the U.S. securities markets has a high degree of cohesion.[2]

From a legal and risk perspective, the interwoven operation in the United States of Article 8 and Article 9 of the Uniform Commercial Code makes for an efficient securities transfer system and facilitates secured lending against investment securities. These statutes, as adopted by each state in the United States, fully recognize the modern indirect holding of securities by investors through one or more brokers or a bank. (Parenthetical citations to the Uniform Commercial Code are included in the following paragraphs for future reference or additional reading.[3])

---

[1]The principal draftsman of this elegant federal structure was James Landis. Landis later ruined his reputation by failing to pay his taxes.

[2]This is not to say that other markets are not cohesive. Most recently, a group of African nations joined in a union of commercial law based in large measure on the Napoleonic Code. The EU's directives are creating a comprehensive framework in Europe, but a true transnational legal regime will not be achieved until PRIMA and UNIDROIT are adopted.

[3]Currently there are close to 5,000 brokers and roughly 8,000 banks in the United States. Of the 8,000 banks, however, only a few hundred provide securities custody services. The lion's share of the brokers rely on clearing brokers to provide custody of their customers' securities.

As securities intermediaries (as defined in Article 8-102), banks and brokers stand between the issuer of securities and the investor. In a world where physical certificates do not exist, the genius of Article 8 and Article 9 was to create the concept of an *entitlement holder* who is a person or entity noted in the bank's or broker's records as the "owner" of securities even though she or it does not possess a certificate. The electronically identified entitlement holder (8-502), according to the statute, possesses a claim to her or its pro rata share of all securities held by the intermediary and consequently to all of the economic and corporate rights associated with that claim (8-503). Specifically, the bank or broker is bound to pass along to the investor payments and distributions (8-505) and voting rights (8-506), and must follow the investor's instructions (8-507), including delivery to the customer of her security if she or it so requests (8-508).[4]

In addition to creating a legal system for the clear delineation of property rights in a certificateless world, Article 8 also clearly sets forth protection for securities intermediaries from adverse claims by persons who might claim their securities had been stolen or otherwise improperly transferred into the intermediary. Absent a court order, collusion or notice that a certificate had been stolen, the intermediary will be protected from a third party trying to claim the security which the intermediary holds on behalf of the investor.[5]

This is critically important for a number of reasons. First, it removes any duty on the intermediary to investigate prior ownership of the security. Processing would grind to a halt if a securities intermediary had to make such an inquiry each time it received a security. Second, the intermediary may, under the dovetailing Article 9, possess its own interest in the investor's security since the customer may not have yet paid for it (in which case the security intermediary has an automatic lien on the security as collateral [9-206 and 9-306]) or the investor may have granted the bank or broker a collateral interest in the security pursuant to a written agreement (9-203). Where the securities intermediary possesses the collateral under a written

---

[4]The DTCC has developed its Direct Registration System (DRS) to provide registered securities owners the ability to hold securities on the records of the transfer agents of issuers in computerized book-entry form. Through DRS, securities can be electronically transferred to and from the transfer agent and broker-dealer. This approach has become the industry norm and all new issues are now required to be DRS eligible effectively eliminating the need for paper certificates. Most listed securities are now DRS eligible. Interestingly, Google, a company whose name is almost synonymous with computers, resisted participation in DRS.

[5]The leading case in the United States on this point is *S.E.C. v. Credit Bancorp*, 386 F.3d 438 (2d cir. 2004).

agreement under which the securities intermediary controls the collateral security (9-106 and 9-314), then, in the event of nonpayment by the investor, the securities intermediary possesses a secured priority (9-328) interest in the collateral and is free to dispose of the collateral to satisfy any debt owed (as long as the broker-dealer or bank does so in a commercially reasonable manner; 9-610). This is true even in the event of the investor's bankruptcy, since the automatic stay of transactions upon a debtor's bankruptcy does not apply in the case of securities accounts.

CUSTODY AND ROOT OF TITLE INTERNATIONALLY

One of the interesting features of securities trading internationally is the diverse approach to defining and establishing ownership of securities. Although the United States may have a comprehensive scheme, other jurisdictions vary widely in their legal concepts as to the holdings of securities through intermediaries.

Root of title is essentially the means by which a person holding securities establishes a link to the underlying security in which formal legal (as opposed to beneficial or economic) title exists. Intermediated holdings are holdings of securities where the account holder does not directly hold legal title himself but has a claim (usually a beneficial or economic interest—although it may be only a contractual interest in certain jurisdictions) against the person who maintains, keeps up, or operates the account recording his interest.

In common law jurisdictions, an account holder would establish a right by means of a claim as beneficiary against the person operating or maintaining such security account in his name. This would not give the account holder a similar right or claim against the next intermediary in the chain. In the example shown in Figure 7.1, A (the investor) has a claim as beneficiary against B (the intermediary) holding in trust for him. B, in turn, has a claim on the basis of a subtrust against C (the custodian), who holds legal title by virtue of his (C's) name appearing on a register of legal title. A has no claim against C in the normal course.

FIGURE 7.1 Common Law Root of Title

FIGURE 7.2 Civil Law Root of Title

In a number of civil jurisdictions, the entitlement of the investor will be established by statute (e.g., Germany or France) such that A must demonstrate that the accounts in which his security interest is recorded are capable of being designated as securities accounts under the relevant statute and, as a result, that he has a co-ownership right in the pool of securities held either by B (where B provides the ultimate root of title) or by reason of an account at C where, although A's contractual relationship is with B, C operates as the source of co-ownership legal rights. (C will be a depository such as Clearstream Banking Frankfurt.) See Figure 7.2.

In certain variations of this model, the account at C, even though C is the ultimate holder or controller of the underlying security, does not grant to C a legal co-ownership right. This right exists only at the level of the account at the first intermediary in the chain beyond C (in this case, B). A will thus have contractual recourse to B and will establish proprietary rights against B, C, and any other person by reference to A's interest being recorded on an account at B. The account at B is being given a special status by reason of its being underpinned by this account at C. In many cases C will hold a security remotely at custodians or in the form of immobilized bearer securities.

In certain markets (e.g., the Netherlands) it is not possible for all of the intermediaries in the chain to confer a proprietary right on the account holder. In the example below, B's account at C establishes a proprietary right of B against C, and against D (the holder of the security) and against any third party. The account at B in A's name gives A no more than a contractual claim against B. On the face of it, A has no proprietary right which it can assert against all parties, only a contractual claim against B.

The range of different treatments of such intermediated securities holdings creates uncertainty in international markets and either real or perceived risks where investors hold securities interests or entitlements subject to laws

FIGURE 7.3 Civil Law Root of Title Variant

with which the investor is not familiar. This uncertainty is addressed by having intermediaries conduct due diligence and ensure that, where available, mechanisms exist so as to provide for effective claims against those other intermediaries or depositories operating or maintaining accounts, including in the event that the person maintaining or operating the account becomes insolvent.

In recent years a number of initiatives have focused on addressing this uncertainty at an international level. Notably, in the EU, an effort is underway to develop a common European approach to establishing the nature of the investors' and each successive intermediary's claim on the next intermediary in the chain so as to ensure not only that it is effective against that intermediary, including in the event of the intermediary's insolvency, but also that it does not cause obligations to be created other than between the investor or intermediary as account holder and the person operating or maintaining the account.[6] The UNIDROIT Convention on Substantive Rules Regarding Intermediated Securities is a similar initiative extending beyond the EU and which the EU project is keen to follow. In short, UNIDROIT seeks to solve the problem by creating one consistent set of rules that would be adopted by all nations.

Other international initiatives, such as The Hague Convention or the Place of Relevant Intermediary Approach (PRIMA), have attempted to establish a common means of determining the law applicable to each account of holding in the chain. This approach would have enabled the account holder and the intermediary to make an effective choice of law that cannot be overturned or, in the absence of a choice of law, select laws based on objective criteria including a location of the person operating the account in order to resolve this issue. The Hague Convention has run into political opposition and is unlikely to be adopted in the near future, at least within the EU. In conclusion, in the absence of uniform law, the international investor is wise to select a well-capitalized custodian.

---

[6]To this end, the EU has proposed the Securities Law Directive (SLD). The SLD sets out minimum requirements for accounts held by EU custodians and subcustodians. In specific, the SLD sets forth standards as to what rights the account holder has (voting, dividends, etc.) and whether these rights can be made conditional. For example, if the securities are held as collateral for a debt, the holder may have fewer rights in them than if there were no debt associated with the holder's securities. When finally promulgated and implemented into national law, a comparison to the U.S. approaches in Article 8 and 9 of the Uniform Commercial Code will prove interesting.

CHAPTER 8

Margin

"Margin" comes from the Latin word meaning *boundary space.* The margin on this page is the space between the edge of the page and the type. Printers always keep a margin so that the typeset does not run off the edge of the paper. Similarly, a broker, when it extends credit, keeps a margin, so that the value of securities collateralizing the loan exceeds the loan amount. The amount of collateral required by the broker above the loan amount is margin. An investor who gives over collateral to a broker-dealer in exchange for a loan from the broker-dealer does so under a margin agreement that allows the broker-dealer to (1) pledge a portion of the securities to a bank in order for the broker-dealer itself to borrow money from the bank with their customers' securities as collateral, or (2) loan out a portion of the securities to a third party. In years gone by, a customer was sometimes allowed, as a matter of custom, to eliminate the broker's right to loan securities to others (thus preventing his own broker from facilitating short sales in the margined stock by third parties). As a matter of practice and regulation, brokers require that margin be posted[1] sufficient to cover the customer's margin debt in the event the collateral needs to be sold to satisfy the loan. Of course, as prices rise and fall, the boundary space for protection must be adjusted.[2]

---

[1]A written agreement is required if securities are to be hypothecated or loaned to others. In addition, the interest rate and how it is calculated must be disclosed. The written agreement, of course, will additionally satisfy the dictates of Article 9 cited in Chapter 7 and gives a broker-dealer control to sell collateral in the event of nonpayment of a margin loan. In the United States, the single best source for the application of extension of credit rules by broker dealers is the *SIA Credit Division Credit Manual,* published by the Securities Industry Association in 2001.

[2]Back when the London Stock Exchange (LSE) operated on a fortnightly settlement, it was possible for an investor to not settle his trade and simply post additional money (called the

On a historical note, one of the conclusions of the Pecora investigation in the aftermath of the 1929 crash was that the loose extension of credit (margin loans) by brokers in the 1920s led to the overvaluation of stocks. Consequently, the extension of credit by banks and brokers to investors to purchase stocks is the subject of strict regulation in the United States. The establishment of strict margin requirements is one of the Federal Reserve's tools to control the money supply. In contrast, the United Kingdom leaves the extension of credit by brokers to their customers as a matter of the brokers' own credit-risk decision making.

The kernel of wisdom to be gleaned from understanding margin loans is the relation to stock lending and the custody of securities. Under the U.S. system, securities not fully paid for, and 140 percent of the market value of securities supporting any margin loan made by a broker, may be pledged or loaned by a broker-dealer to itself or others. It is by this means that brokers can borrow stock to satisfy a settlement obligation or can facilitate short selling through the loan of securities to the short seller's broker. Therefore, in addition to earning interest on its secured margin loans, a broker-dealer makes an additional return on its stock loan operations. A more complete explanation follows in Chapter 9.

---

contango if he was long and called the *backwardation* of he was short). In either case, the broker was liable to the market to settle the trade or risk being bought in by the market if so directed by the LSE. See Francis W. Hirst, *The Stock Exchange: A Short History of Investment and Speculation* 4th ed. (Oxford University Press 1948).

Short Selling and Stock Loans

S elling securities one does not own for future delivery (short selling) in the hope that the securities sold will decline in price and be acquired cheaper than the original sale price has been around at least as long as modern markets.[1] Stock lending as a means to facilitate settlement or cover short sales does not have such a long history. In fact, it was the development of the listed options market in the United States in the 1970s that increased demand for securities to facilitate settlement in the 1960s, and the growth of the prime brokerage business in the 1980s that led to the growth of securities lending.

Now, securities lending, done pursuant to standardized agreements, is a principal means of finance (through repurchase transactions)[2] and the principal vehicle to facilitate short selling and settlement.[3]

In the United States, the Federal Reserve's Regulation T establishes the permitted purposes for which a broker-dealer may borrow securities. One such purpose allows brokers to borrow securities to complete deliveries. The broker-dealer can call other brokers or lending banks (which act as agents) to locate the needed securities. If the broker-dealer borrows the

---

[1]Daniel Drew is perhaps one of the most famous short sellers in history. After the U.S. Civil War, Drew (for whom Drew University in New Jersey is named) attempted to short Erie Railroad stock and gain a profit at the expense of Cornelius Vanderbilt. Drew's scheme, which ultimately was frustrated by Vanderbilt, Jay Gould, and Jim Fisk, led to the quip, "He who sells what isn't his'n, must buy it back or go to prison." Charles Francis Adams Jr. and Henry Adams, *Chapters of Erie* (Waveland Press 2002), describe the manipulations by Daniel Drew of Erie Railroad stock.

[2]Sometimes referred to as *cash-driven* securities lending. Samples of Standard Master Repurchase Agreements can be found at www.sifma.org and from the International Capital Markets Association, www.icmagroup.org.

[3]Sometimes referred to as *securities-driven* lending. Samples of a Master Stock Loan Agreement can be found at www.sifma.org and at the International Securities Lending Association, www.isla.co.uk.

JUSTICE ON THE RAIL—ERIE RAILROAD (RING) SMASH UP.

THE OVERTHROW OF THE ERIE RING

The downfall of Daniel Drew and his confederates, having been caught short.
Source: Courtesy of Cartoonstock, Ltd. Reproduced with permission.

securities from another broker, the broker-dealer borrowing the securities will give collateral (usually cash) to the lending broker. The lending broker is permitted to invest the cash collateral and keep the interest income earned on the cash collateral investment. If the broker-dealer is borrowing the securities from an agent-lending bank, the bank typically invests the cash collateral on behalf of the true beneficial owner of the loaned stock (i.e., a mutual fund, pension fund, college endowment fund, or other custodial client of the agent bank that participates in the agent bank's lending program). In both cases, the borrowing broker may ask to share in the income generated from the cash collateral reinvestment earned by the securities lender. If the lender chooses to share this income, the interest paid to the borrower is called a rebate.

Typically, if the stock or bond being borrowed is readily available and in large supply ("easy to borrow"), the lender will share the majority of the cash collateral reinvestment income, keeping (on average) 50 basis points for itself. However, if the securities being borrowed are not readily available, or if the securities are in great demand when compared to supply, the borrower may get none of the cash collateral reinvestment income, and in fact might have to pay the lender an additional interest rate to borrow "hard to borrow" securities. This additional interest is called a *negative rebate*.

A third source of securities for the borrowing broker may be its own principal trading inventory, and a fourth may be the margin holdings of its retail customers. Retail customers who purchase securities on margin sign a margin agreement, which allows the carrying broker to rehypothecate[4] (essentially borrow) unpaid-for shares from the customer. Regulation T allows the broker-dealer to borrow any securities from the customer up to a market value of 140 percent of the customer debit balance. For example, if a customer bought 1,000 shares of IBM at $100 per share, Regulation T requires the customer to pay for half of the purchase, or $50,000. The broker-dealer can lend the customer the other $50,000. The broker-dealer can rehypothecate $70,000 ($50,000 debit × 140 percent) worth of securities. The reason the broker-dealer is allowed to "borrow" shares worth more than the customer owes is because the banks that might lend money to the broker-dealer (should the broker-dealer choose to pledge the IBM shares for a bank loan) only advance the broker-dealer $0.70 for every $1 of collateral pledged. Therefore, Regulation T allows the broker-dealer to finance the money it lends to its customers and assumes the broker-dealer would have to borrow money from a bank to do so.

---

[4]The word hypothecate is often used interchangeably in the securities industry to mean both *pledge* and *stock loan*. In its most precise sense, hypothecation is a pledge of securities. The customer "hypothecates" his securities to the broker for the margin loan. The word comes from the Greek *hypo*, meaning *under*, and *theca*, meaning *receptacle*. The words convey the meaning of a portion of property safely segregated for the benefit of a lender. Richard Whitney, one-time President of the New York Stock Exchange, famously misused his customer securities by pledging them to a bank without his customer's consent and then stole the loan proceeds. It was a scandal that rocked the Wall Street establishment and Whitney went to jail. The incident occurred before the safeguards described in Chapter 15.

If the broker-dealer chooses to use rehypothecated shares to complete the delivery, the "borrowed" shares do not leave the customer's account; rather, the broker-dealer is allowed to simply deliver the unpaid-for shares. To ensure the broker-dealer does not use more shares than permitted, a nightly margin calculation is performed for all customer accounts. The broker's margin system will identify which securities are fully paid for by each customer and which are not. The paid-for securities are segregated on the books and records of the broker. The unpaid-for securities are unsegregated and are freely available for the broker-dealer to use to make deliveries or pledge to lending banks. If a margin customer pays off its debit balance, the margin system will identify all the securities in the customer account as fully paid for and the broker-dealer will have to re-obtain any and all securities it might have rehypothecated from the customer's account. If the broker-dealer does not have possession of the fully paid-for customer shares, the broker-dealer must set aside its own capital (130 percent of the market value of the deficient shares) to protect the customer, and place these funds in a special deposit account reserved for the benefit of its customers. The broker-dealer may borrow these deficient shares from another internal margin customer, its own inventory, or a lending broker or agent bank.

In all cases, when a broker-dealer borrows securities, the majority of the rights of ownership stay with the securities lender. The lender is entitled to receive all dividends and income on the securities loaned. However, the tax treatment for these payments is changed. The lender receives a "substitute payment" from the borrower in an amount equal to the dividend or interest payment. The reason the lender does not receive the actual dividend is because the actual holder of the securities on the record date will receive the dividend. Imagine a customer sells short 100 shares of a stock. The broker-dealer borrows 100 shares to make the delivery to the buyer. If a $0.15 per share dividend is paid, the buyer gets paid the "real" dividend since the buyer is also the holder of the stock. The borrower needs to pay the lender the cash amount of the dividend in the form of a substitute payment and gets that money from the short seller. To further the example and explain its fairness, when the stock started trading ex-dividend, the price of the stock dropped by $0.15. This is logical for the lender and the buyer, as they are receiving compensation of the $0.15 per share in the form of the dividend. The short seller would realize a profit of $0.15 per share if the dividend money were not charged to its account.

Similarly, the stock lender loses the right to vote loaned shares in event of a proxy solicitation. Following the one-share, one-vote concept, the lender cannot vote what is not in its possession. Using the same example as given

Capital raising by the issuance of stock supported the early
development of railroads and canals.

previously, the buyer-holder who is in possession of the stock is entitled to
vote the shares. The lender cannot vote and, unlike the dividend-substitute
payment scenario, cannot simply get the vote from the borrower. The borrower cannot "give" the vote or vote on the lender's behalf because it cannot
obtain the vote from the short seller (unlike the ability to simply charge cash
to the short seller).[5]

---

[5]Many firms actually reduce the customer's vote before the proxy solicitation process begins
to reflect the fact that shares had been lent out over the voting record date. The practice is
called "pre-balancing." Some firms may reduce votes after a customer has voted as part of a
reconciliation of votes received to shares actually custodied by the firm. Note: If a customer
wants to fully vote her holdings, she must have fully paid for those shares over the record date.

If a lender wants or needs its loaned securities back, it can recall the securities from the borrower (unless, of course, the loan is a term loan that has not yet reached maturity). Failure to return the loaned securities within the recall period (typically three settlement days, although this is variable by contract) means that the lender may purchase the unreturned securities in the open market using the collateral posted by the borrower and charging the borrower for any cost over and above the collateral sold/used to repurchase the securities (or may keep the collateral in settlement).

Securities lending and borrowing requires a signed master securities lending agreement between both parties prior to any loans being executed. In recent years other products have been created to emulate the basic economics of a securities lending transaction. Total return swaps and contracts for difference (discussed in Chapter 10) are two such "derivatives" of securities loans.

Controversial though it may be, the truth is that short selling is as natural as the farmer who sells his crop before the crops have been harvested. Although few can deny the advantages in liquidity that short selling brings to a marketplace, many jurisdictions prohibit the practice or enforce strict "buy-in" rules in the event a seller fails to deliver a security to the buyer.

CHAPTER 10

Derivatives

D erivatives such as futures, forwards, swaps, and options are important since they redistribute risks generated in the real economy, and are accordingly important tools for economic agents to transfer risk. They can be used for insuring against risk (hedging). However, investors have increasingly used derivatives to gain a purely economic exposure to the underlying asset or market variable with the aim of making a profit (speculation). An important feature of derivatives is that they allow those who use them to obtain leverage: With a relatively small outlay, the investor is able to take a large position in the market.

THE OTC DERIVATIVE MARKETS

Derivatives are traded on formal exchanges or in a person-to-person or over-the-counter (OTC) basis that does not involve a formal exchange. Instead, participants trade directly with each other. Traditionally, OTC trades, just as with most bond trading, have been concluded over the phone (voice brokerage) but are increasingly taking place on electronic networks (e.g., between dealers or between dealers and their clients).

OTC derivatives are simply derivatives traded on OTC markets. Their main difference from the derivatives traded on exchanges lies in their highly individualized nature; whereas on-exchange derivatives are traded on standard terms (e.g., there is a limited choice of strike prices or maturities that can be traded), OTC derivatives are nonstandardized, offering full flexibility in deciding those terms.[1] They are accordingly

---

[1] In simple terms, the difference has been likened to the difference between a bus and a taxi. A bus has a schedule with set stops and a regular route; a taxi takes you directly to your

tailor-made to fit the specific risk management and other specific needs of investors.

Formerly, there were many derivatives that were traded in the OTC markets and were subject to less regulation than was true for exchange-traded derivatives. In the United States, the Dodd-Frank financial reforms have made significant changes in this area. Now, many more derivatives will need to be cleared through central clearing systems and traded on recognized exchanges.

Why Are OTC Derivatives Markets Regarded as More Risky than Exchange-Traded Derivatives Markets?

OTC markets are characterized by bilateral contracting between counterparties, with each counterparty taking on the credit risk of the other party. The bilateral nature of these markets creates a complex web of mutual dependence between counterparties. Coupled with the markets' opaqueness, this creates a situation in which it is difficult for market participants and regulators to understand fully the true nature and level of risks that any particular market participant is exposed to. This increases uncertainty in times of market stress and can accordingly undermine financial stability as has been clearly illustrated by the recent financial crisis.

The Role Derivatives Played in the 2008–2009 Financial Crisis

Although OTC derivatives markets were not responsible for the onset of the crisis, they played both a direct and an indirect role in its propagation. The direct role was epitomized by the near collapse of AIG due to its dealings in the credit default swaps market. The indirect role had more to do with the participants in those markets. Bear Stearns and Lehman Brothers, two of the institutions swept away by the crisis, were important players in the OTC

---

destination. Both are good forms of transportation depending on the rider's needs. Typically, derivatives contracts are negotiated by using standard forms developed by the International Swaps and Derivatives Association, www.isda.org.

derivatives markets, as either dealers or users of OTC derivatives, or both, although many other factors were at play in the demise of those institutions.

LEGAL DEFINITION OF DERIVATIVES

Derivatives are financial instruments whose value is derived from the value of an underlying asset (e.g., the price of an equity, bond, or commodity) or market variable (e.g., an interest rate, an exchange rate, or a stock index). The main types of derivatives are futures, options, and swaps. Options, particularly listed options, are well known in the United States and Europe and will not be covered in any depth in this book. A central counterparty, the Options Clearing Corporation, and various exchanges, notably the Chicago Board Option Exchange, support the trading of U.S.-listed options. LIFFE and Eurex perform similar functions in the United Kingdom and Europe. Another type of derivative, the credit derivative, takes its value from underlying assets like loans, bonds, and other forms of credit. The main type of credit derivative is the Credit Default Swap (CDS). Given its prominence in the most recent financial collapse, we examine briefly CDS. Then we look at another popular derivative, the contract for difference (CFD), because—like listed options—CFDs are popular with retail investors.[2]

WHAT IS A CDS?

A CDS is in many ways similar to an insurance contract. In exchange for paying an annual premium, the CDS buyer (i.e., the protection buyer) is insured against losses caused by a credit event (e.g., a default) related to the debt of a specific reference entity (e.g., a company or a bank).

The analogy with an insurance contract stops here: The protection buyer does not need to own the underlying debt in order to be able to purchase the CDS. However, to be able to collect the "insurance" payment from the CDS seller (i.e., the protection seller) in case a credit event does occur,

---

[2]For more information on the derivatives market, including an in-depth discussion of futures, options, and the various types of swaps refer to Robert Kolb and James Overdahl, *Futures, Options and Swaps* 5th ed. (John Wiley & Sons 2007).

the protection buyer must deliver an equivalent amount of the debt (bonds or loans) of the reference entity to the protection seller.

What Is a Credit Event?

A credit event is an event that may trigger the exercise of a CDS contract. Typically, credit events include failure to pay (interest or principal when due), bankruptcy, or restructuring.

Why Have CDSs Been Singled Out as Particularly Risky?

Credit derivatives markets are built on products that bind together institutions and markets in ways that are difficult to understand and survey, both at the institutional and systemic level. CDSs are relatively small compared to other OTC derivatives markets, but they are particularly significant in terms of risk.

The CDS market is highly concentrated among a handful of banks. A failure of any of them can have severe implications for the CDS market and for financial markets as a whole, as the Lehman bankruptcy and near failure of AIG in September 2008 demonstrated.

The total gross notional amount of outstanding CDSs is a multiple of the total amount of underlying debt on which these contracts were written. The payoff of a CDS is discontinuous. In exchange for a continuous stream of revenue from the protection buyer, the protection seller assumes the risk of having to pay out the full amount of the insurance if the reference entity on which the CDS is written defaults. As the revenue he receives is usually but a fraction of the payment that he would need to make, he is exposed to the risk of incurring a substantial loss in case a default does occur.

Contracts are nonfungible. Because of this, market participants that wish to close a position can only do so by going back to the original counterparty (usually a dealer) or by entering into an offsetting contract with a different counterparty. In the latter case, the net exposure of the participant is reduced to zero. However, the risk associated with the two contracts is not completely removed, as counterparty risk remains (if one of the counterparties defaulted, the hedge would be undone). This is why gross exposure matters.

Pricing CDSs is difficult. Compared to interest rate swaps, where risks are well understood and contracts rely on widely available and tested data for their pricing (e.g., share prices, interest rates, exchange rates), the data needed to price CDSs (e.g., firms' balance sheets) is more scarce and often less authoritative. Therefore, the probability of mispricing CDSs is higher than is the case with other types of derivatives.

Why Is Standardization Necessary?

Conducting trades under the framework of widely adopted, standard contractual terms increases legal certainty and reduces legal risk. Moreover, standardization increases operational efficiency, as it enables automating the structure of the trading and post-trading value chain. Standardization may also reduce counterparty credit risk, as it enables a wider usage of CCP clearing or exchange trading. Standardization is accordingly a *sine qua non* for delivering efficient, safe, and sound derivatives markets. The U.S. experience in listed options since the 1970s is evidence that a standardized model with an exchange and CCP works.

In the U.S., the Dodd-Frank reforms have introduced clearing and exchange trading requirements on the CDS market as well as many formerly lightly regulated derivatives. These reforms should generate greater transparency to the markets and promote greater contract standardization, all of which should promote a healthier and less systemically risky environment for these instruments.

What Is a Central Data Repository?

A central data repository collects data on contracts traded in one or more segments of the OTC derivatives markets (both CCP eligible and CCP noneligible). Through a central data repository one can therefore obtain information on, for example, the number of outstanding contracts, the size of outstanding positions in a particular contract, and so on. This not only contributes to transparency, but also improves the operational efficiency of the market. A repository can also provide other services (e.g., facilitate settlement and payment instructions).

A data repository exists for CDSs in the form of the Trade Information Warehouse, operated by the DTCC. The Dodd-Frank reforms have mandated that the SEC and CFTC develop additional data repositories as well as derivatives clearing systems, both private and public.

CONTRACT FOR DIFFERENCE (CFD)

A popular investment for speculators in the United Kingdom (but little understood in the United States) is a contract for difference. Its features and uses are explained next.

Background Material

A contract for difference (CFD) is a derivative contract that allows the two parties to that contract—a buyer and a seller—to exchange the cash difference between the opening price and the closing price of that contract in a given security and/or index (the underlying asset) upon the closing out of that transaction. A CFD, therefore, allows an investor to express a view of the markets, by taking either long or short positions to gain exposure to the price movement of stocks and indices, and all this without owning the underlying asset itself or paying a stamp tax associated with owning the underlying security. In contrast to listed stock options, there is no expiration date. The essential requirement to a CFD is that a holder post sufficient margin to keep the position open.

CFDs are widely believed to have originated in London in the early 1990s, born out of a desire by some institutional investors to short equities without having to undergo the cumbersome processes associated with repurchase and stock-lending transactions. Proving again that there is nothing new under the sun, CFDs functionally are much like contracts sold in the United States by so-called *bucket shops* at the end of the nineteenth century and in the early twentieth century in the United States. In those arrangements, speculators would enter into the same kind of arrangement as a modern CFD with a broker. Because of the sharp practices of these dealers, bucket shops became a term of derision and the type of contract was, and still is, not permitted in the United States.

Although CFDs can, from the investor's point of view, replicate the economic benefits of owning the underlying asset, there remain important distinctions between trading a CFD and trading the underlying asset.

A CFD is traded on margin, unlike the underlying asset. Trades require the investor to lodge collateral with the CFD provider, and this collateral encompasses both initial and variation margin to cover any volatility in the price of the underlying asset and any calculations that reflect an increased leverage.

The investor in a CFD product does not own the underlying stock, but only enters into an agreement with the counterparty to exchange the cash difference in price between the opening and closing price of the transaction.

A CFD can be traded long as well as short, and there is no need for delivery of the underlying asset.

A CFD is one of the few OTC derivatives products that offer trading opportunities, across the spectrum, to all retail and institutional investors, including hedge funds and other market participants. CFDs have achieved immense popularity in London and elsewhere overseas among both retail and institutional investors, mainly because they:

- Provide valuable U.K. tax incentives, as they are exempt from the U.K. government stamp duty tax of 0.5 percent. Stamp duty is usually levied on equity trades.
- Are not currently, and have not been historically, subject to stringent disclosure rules like stock transfers.
- Offer the investor the ability to short an underlying instrument, and, as opposed to repurchase and stock lending transactions, the investor does not undertake an obligation to physically deliver the underlying asset.
- Offer leverage to the price movements of a large number of underlying instruments, because CFDs are margined products.

LEGAL AND REGULATORY FRAMEWORK OF CFDS

In the United Kingdom, CFDs have until recently remained outside the regulatory framework governing stock holdings disclosure requirements under the Financial Services Authority's (FSA) Disclosure and Transparency Rules (DTR). As in the case of single-stock futures, long CFD holders could, if the contract allows, convert their CFD holdings into physical ownership of the underlying stock on closing of the contract. As a result of this happenstance, the FSA identified three issues that might arise from nondisclosure by investors of CFDs that they hold. These are the occurrence of:

- Inefficient price formation
- A distorted market for takeovers
- Diminished market confidence

To this end, the FSA has been eager to ensure that holders of long CFD positions, especially by institutional investors, abide by measures that will, among other things, bring transparency and enhance investor protection in the capital markets.

Following back-and-forth consultations by the FSA with the wider financial services industry, amid concerns on the part of the FSA that CFD holders could potentially stealthily build up equity stakes in a company without the company in question knowing, the FSA has promulgated new rules which would require disclosure of long CFD positions, which aggregate a total holding of 3 percent or more of the issuer company's total shareholding. This new disclosure regime for long-held CFDs amends the DTR and is enshrined in the Disclosure and Transparency Rules (Disclosure of Contracts for Differences) Instrument 2009. The new rules came into force on June 1, 2009.

As mentioned above, the United States has still not approved CFDs for sale to U.S. persons, whether retail or institutional. CFDs have historically run up against the U.S. notion that they are fundamentally wagering contracts. Arguments were raised in the past that CFDs should not be considered commodity futures or OTC derivatives falling within the CFTC's jurisdiction, but those arguments have largely lost steam as a result of the provisions of the CFTC Reauthorization Act of 2008, which clarified that the CFTC's jurisdiction extends to OTC futures and forwards, and presumably CFDs as well (although CFDs are not explicitly addressed in the legislation).

THE OUTLOOK FOR CFDs

The CFD market in the United Kingdom has grown significantly in the past five years. Recently, figures from the FSA indicated that about 30 percent of equity trades were in some way driven by CFD transactions where the CFDs referenced the underlying shares in question.

The global outlook for CFDs also looks increasingly promising even though they are not yet approved in the United States. Even though traditionally CFDs have been traded off-exchange as OTC derivative products, they have for a long time now been accessible to a wide range of investors, including retail investors. This is attributable to innovations in electronic trading systems in the late 1990s, which allowed retail investors the opportunity to trade CFDs on London Stock Exchange (LSE) stocks.

Since 2007, the Australian Stock Exchange (ASX) has afforded further opportunity to retail investors to trade CFDs by creating an exchange-listed CFD product—a product listed on a separate market on the ASX. There are attempts in the United Kingdom, although these have been put on hold for an indefinite period, to also create an exchange-listed CFD product on the LSE. The added attractions of exchange-listed CFDs are obvious, as all trades will be guaranteed by a CCP, thereby significantly lessening counterparty risk exposure and also providing a depth of liquidity.

CHAPTER 11

Prime Brokerage

In its most generic sense, prime brokerage refers to an investment firm acting as custodian and lender where the investment firm is not the sole place where the customer executes his securities transactions. In exchange, the prime broker secures the right to lend the customer's securities. As we have seen, the lending of securities by brokerage firms in the United States is a matter of tight credit regulation pursuant to Regulation T. In other countries, most notably the United Kingdom, firms are free to extend credit as they see fit as long as they are prudent. This more relaxed standard is one of the reasons for the phenomenal growth of the hedge fund industry in the United Kingdom. In the United States, prime brokerage has a much more specific meaning and regulatory framework because prime brokers must fit within the dictates of Regulation T and specific dictates of the SEC. A short history will help explain the U.S. model, which can be contrasted with prime brokerages around the world.

In the past, when hedge funds wanted research from wire houses, the funds could pay directly for the information (which they generally did not want to do) or they could establish accounts at the wire houses and transact purchases and sales with these providers. The wire houses would make a commission or a mark-up on the trades in lieu of a direct payment and thereby get paid (in soft dollars) for the research they provided. This resulted in hedge funds having accounts at every brokerage firm from which they purchased research. You can imagine the effort required by the hedge fund to consolidate these widespread accounts and the additional efforts to manage margin calls and collateral between multiple brokerage firms and accounts. From this, the concept of having a single "prime" broker evolved.

The prime broker became the single "carrying" broker where the hedge fund could consolidate its assets (long and short holdings). This consolidation allowed the hedge fund to manage its cash and securities holdings better, and gave it more bargaining power with its single provider. In a prime brokerage relationship, the hedge fund continues to trade with other firms, paying commissions to the executing broker (often in exchange for research). For each and every trade executed away from the hedge fund's prime broker, the executing broker and the prime broker book a "trade" between themselves on behalf of the hedge fund, thereby moving the executing broker's trade for the hedge fund to the books of the prime broker. The hedge fund (and indirectly its investors) also reaped the benefit of receiving from the prime broker one monthly consolidated statement, thereby allowing for easier reconciliation, and so on.[1]

By way of example, a hedge fund gives an order to an executing broker to buy 1,000 shares of IBM. The executing broker fills the order, buying IBM on the NYSE at $99 per share. The executing broker charges the hedge fund a $150 commission and places the buy trade in a broker-dealer credit account designated for the benefit of the hedge fund customer.[2] The broker-dealer credit account has delivery instructions to the hedge fund's prime broker. The executing broker sends an ID confirmation to the hedge fund's prime broker. The hedge fund informs its prime broker of the execution, and the prime broker effects a purchase into the account of the hedge fund and affirms the ID notice sent by the executing broker. On the settlement date the executing broker's market purchase settles, with the executing broker paying the seller $99,000. The executing broker delivers the 1,000 shares to the prime broker against receipt of $99,150 (keeping the $150 commission). The prime broker receives the 1,000 shares into the hedge fund's account and debits the hedge fund for the cost of the purchase ($99,150).

If the securities being traded and the brokers involved in the transaction are all NSCC/CNS-eligible for comparison and netting, *and* all the legs of the trade were submitted and compared timely (prior to 12 P.M. on T+2),

---

[1]This model of operation required certain concessions from the SEC. See SEC No-Action letter of January 25, 1994, to SIA Prime Broker Committee.

[2]The broker-dealer credit account was used in order to avoid the strictures of Regulation T, which would not allow the delivery of securities by one broker dealer to the customer of another broker dealer without a "letter of free funds." Prior to the adoption of the 1994 No-Action letter referenced in the previous footnote, the executing firm would need a letter indicating the receiving broker had sufficient funds on hand from its customer to pay for the trade done at the executing broker before the broker could agree to deliver the shares purchased by the customer to the receiving broker for custody. This was a cumbersome process eliminated by the use of the broker-dealer credit account. Broker-dealers are free to settle trades between themselves on a good faith basis. The procedure was ratified by the 1994 No-Action letter.

the prime broker would be receiving the shares purchased by the hedge fund from NSCC/CNS against payment of the $99,150. The selling broker would owe the shares to NSCC/CNS against payment of $99,000, and the executing broker would have no delivery or receive obligations and NSCC/CNS would credit its account $150.

Prior to an executing broker's taking an order from a hedge fund that has a prime broker, the prime broker and the executing broker would sign an agreement where the prime broker would list all of its hedge fund clients who have or might have permission to trade with the executing broker. The list of hedge funds at the prime broker is detailed on Schedule A to the agreement (known in the prime brokerage community as Form 150). Frequently, the prime broker takes on new (or loses) hedge fund customers. When this happens the prime broker sends a notice to the executing broker notifying it of the modification to the Schedule A. This notice is called a Form 1 to Schedule A. The executing broker would confirm the prime broker's commitment to the hedge fund(s) by signing the Schedule A (or Form 1 to Schedule A). This commitment indicates that the prime broker will back the hedge fund clients' trades for settlement, allowing the executing broker to treat the trades as "broker-dealer credit" trades (a direct obligation of the prime broker). The prime broker has 24 hours after notification of an execution from the executing broker to *DK* ("Don't Know" meaning to disaffirm) the trade and/or disown the hedge fund. The latter would only occur if the hedge fund and the prime broker have severed their relationship (which is typically followed by a deletion of the hedge fund from the prime broker's Schedule A). If the prime broker does not deny recognizing the ID notification (referred to as DKing), the prime broker is contractually obligated to take responsibility for the trade (just as if it had proactively acknowledged the trade).

Over the years, hedge funds have grown primarily as traders and the prime broker structure has allowed traders to leave wire houses and strike out on their own. The trading strategies have become sophisticated and continue to become more exotic with the proliferation of derivative products. Concurrently, prime brokers have also become savvy and catered to the hedge funds by designing these products for the hedge fund market. Many hedge funds fear that their prime brokers will piggyback their trading ideas or front-run them, thereby diluting the market opportunities available. To combat this fear, larger hedge funds now employ multiple prime brokers and split their strategies among them. This is somewhat counter to the whole intent of creating the prime brokerage system and obtaining approval from

Scrip for the payment of stock.

the SEC, but it affords the hedge funds some strategic cover. However, each prime broker needs to be comfortable with the risk and leverage it provides to a hedge fund without regard to what the hedge fund might be doing with other prime brokers. This is best evidenced by the failure of Long Term Capital Management in 1998, which had leveraged its assets to a great degree and was forced to sell its holdings when the assets in its portfolios had little to no market liquidity.[3]

---

[3]The tale of the demise of Long Term Capital is told by Roger Lowenstein in *When Genius Failed: The Rise and Fall of Long-Term Capital Management* (Random House 2001). Straightforward advice for hedge funds can be found in the *Hedge Fund Deskbook, Legal and Practical Advice for a New Era*, by Morgan, Lewis & Bockius (West 2009).

CHAPTER 12

Managed Accounts

It is safe to say that in 1973, when E.F. Hutton client Hilda Peck opened the *first* separately managed account (SMA),[1] no one could have predicted the extraordinary popularity and growth that SMAs would achieve over the next 35 years. Indeed, the structure and tax planning benefits of SMAs have contributed to an industry that today controls approximately $1,332.3 ($billions) in assets[2] and boasts an ever-expanding array of products.

The acknowledged founder of the SMA industry, Jim Lockwood, originally conceived the SMA concept when he was a retail stockbroker who was consulting in the institutional defined benefit pension market, introducing money managers to pension funds and, in return, receiving directed trades from the managers of these funds.[3] May Day 1975, when negotiated commission rates were introduced, spurred Lockwood on and he created the first wrap fee program, with "a professionally managed portfolio, run at an all-inclusive 3% fee. By negotiating the commission rates to zero cents per share, and charging an advisory fee, the broker's interests became aligned with the clients."[4]

---

[1]See Sydney LeBlanc, *Legacy: The History of Separately Managed Accounts* (MMI 2002). These products are referred to also as individually managed accounts, separate accounts, managed accounts, fee-based accounts and managed money. See also Stephen D. Gresham, *The Managed Account Handbook* (Connecticut River Press 2002).

[2]Cerulli Associates, *The Cerulli Edge* (2Q 2009).

[3]Leonard Reinhart, 2010: "A Managed Account Odyssey: Projections on the Future of the Individually Managed Account Industry" (January 2002).

[4]*Id.* At the time, Lockwood was quoted as saying, "As always is the case in an efficient capitalist system, once rates are no longer protected by a 'cartel' [NYSE], the rates don't go up, they go down. And, over time, that revenue stream becomes less and less reliable because competition will ultimately drive it to the lowest cost service provider. So the ability to earn a premium income by rendering advice through commission revenue stream was not something to bet your long-term livelihood on." LeBlanc, *supra* note 1, at 8.

As a general description, SMA programs have evolved to be defined as "programs by which asset managers manage investors' assets in discretionary separate accounts. A bundled asset-based fee (often 2.5% to 3% before breakpoints and discounts from negotiation) covers money management, trading and custody."[5] Put differently, instead of a broker managing a client's money on a discretionary basis an investor gets an umbrella structure in the form of an investment advisor, which has associated within it an array of investment advisors that the client can choose from to manage his assets. For this service, he pays one fee, instead of brokerage commissions, and is advantaged by having made available to him a number of investment advisors and styles.[6]

HISTORY OF RULE 3A-4

Although the first SMA was opened in 1973 and the first full SMA program (E.F. Hutton Select Managers program) was launched by Jim Lockwood at E.F. Hutton in 1987, it was not until March 24, 1997, that the SEC adopted Rule 3a-4 under the 1940 Act (Rule 3a-4) to provide a nonexclusive safe harbor from the definition of the term *investment company* for certain programs under which investment advisory services are provided on a discretionary basis to a large number of advisory clients having relatively small amounts to invest.[7] Rule 3a-4 continues today as the governing structure for SMA programs; compliance with the rule allows SMA programs to avoid registration as a mutual fund under the 1940 Act.

The SEC originally proposed a precursor to Rule 3a-4 in 1980, "which would have provided a safe harbor for investment management services affording clients individualized treatment. The rule was not adopted at that time due to public opposition."[8] Between 1980 and 1995 (when the SEC

---

[5]Cerulli Associates, "The Cerulli Edge Managed Account Edition" (1Q 2007).

[6]The beauty of the structure is that a money manager is fed assets to manage that he otherwise might not have obtained, but for them having been presented to him through the program. The investor, by being presented to the manager as part of the larger structure, which includes other investors, gets a professional money manager who, without the benefit of the program, might not have taken him on as a client.

[7]SEC Final Release No. IC-22579; IA-1623; S7-24-95 62 Fed. Reg. 15098 (March 31, 1997, 1997 release). See also MMI Technical Bulletin dated April 4, 1997.

[8]Steven W. Stone, "Wrap Fee Programs and Separately Managed Accounts" (June 17, 2009).

reproposed Rule 3a-4), the SEC staff "issued a number of no-action letters that were based, in large part, on representations that the programs would comply with the proposed [1980 version] of Rule 3a-4."[9] Although this is an unusual trajectory in the world of securities regulation, the SEC has over time provided substantial guidance on the structure of SMA programs and related issues through no-action letters.

In 1997, at the time Rule 3a-4 was adopted, the SEC summarized the new rule's requirements as follows:

- Each client's account must be managed on the basis of the client's financial situation and investment objectives, and in accordance with any reasonable restrictions imposed by the client on the management of the account.
- The sponsor of the program must obtain sufficient information from each client to be able to provide individualized investment advice to the client.
- The sponsor and portfolio manager must be reasonably available to consult with each client.
- Each client must have the ability to impose reasonable restrictions on the management of the client's account.
- Each client must be provided with a quarterly account statement containing a description of all activities in the client's account.
- Each client must retain certain indicia of ownership of all securities and funds in the account.[10]

The rule applies to discretionary advisory programs only.

Under Rule 3a-4, the "sponsor" of a program is "any person who receives compensation for sponsoring, organizing or administering the program, or for selecting, or providing advice regarding the selection of persons responsible for managing the client's account in the program."[11]

---

[9] Dechert Price & Rhoads, Investment Management Client Memo No. 97-8 (July 2, 1997); see also Stone, supra note 8, at n.5 (citing, e.g., Wall Street Preferred Money Managers, April 10, 1992); Rauscher Pierce Refsnes, Inc. (April 10, 1992); Westfield Consultants Group (December 13, 1991); Atlantic Bank of New York (June 7, 1991).

[10] 1997 Release.

[11] Rule 3a-4 under the Investment Company Act of 1940.

APPLICABILITY OF THE ADVISERS ACT

A sponsor of a wrap fee or SMA program[12] usually meets the definition of "investment adviser"[13] under the Advisers Act and is required to be registered with the SEC. The Advisers Act defines a wrap fee program as "a program under which any client is charged a specified fee or fees not based directly upon transactions in a client's account for investment advisory services (which may include portfolio management or advice concerning the selection of other investment advisers) and execution of client transactions."[14] Each money manager in a wrap fee program is also generally registered as an investment adviser, unless subject to an applicable exemption, such as a bank would be.

Both the sponsor of an SMA program and a money manager participating in the program have significant disclosure obligations under the Advisers Act.

In 1994 the SEC adopted Rule 204-3(f) under the Advisers Act, requiring sponsors of SMA programs to provide investor clients with a disclosure brochure, called a Schedule H.[15] The Schedule H includes a detailed description of the SMA program, including the services provided, fees charged, and the sponsor's practices relating to the selection and retention of portfolio managers, to name a few. The Schedule H must be delivered to investor clients initially before entering into a contract, and a supplement must be delivered annually thereafter and at such times as material changes are made to the disclosure document. Each money manager in an SMA program generally must also provide the investor client with a disclosure document, at the same frequency applicable to a sponsor. It should be noted that a money manager's disclosure document is contained in the manager's Form ADV.

---

[12] The terms *separately managed account program* and *wrap fee program* are not defined in Rule 3a-4. The Money Management Institute (MMI) defines a traditional SMA program as a "single account that corresponds to a single investment strategy. To hold multiple strategies, a client must open multiple accounts. These programs include all the attributes of 'managed account solutions' such as client profiling, fee-based pricing and research and includes SMA dual contract programs" (MMI Central, 2Q 2009).

[13] 1997 Release at 5.

[14] Rule 204-3(f) under the Advisers Act.

[15] The Schedule H is a schedule to the Form ADV, which is the registration form for SEC-registered investment advisers.

CURRENT SMA EXAM ISSUES

As registered investment advisers, both sponsors and money managers are subject to regular examinations by securities regulators. In recent years, the SEC has focused on the following issues in its examination of SMA programs:

- Best execution
- Suitability
- Fee calculations
- Disclosures
- Rule 3a-4 compliance[16]

The issue of best execution has become a significant focus of regulators. Investment advisers are required to act in the best interest of their advisory clients. Part of that obligation includes obtaining the best price and execution for their securities transactions. The SEC defines "best execution" as "seeking the best price for a security in the marketplace as well as ensuring that, in executing client transactions clients do not incur unnecessary brokerage costs and charges. To seek to obtain best execution, advisers must periodically evaluate the execution performance of the broker-dealers they use to execute client transactions."[17] Two of the most common deficiencies found by the SEC in the area of best execution are (1) inadequate internal controls related to brokerage arrangement and execution, and (2) failure to disclose conflicts of interests related to brokerage arrangements.

Both sponsors of SMA programs and money managers in SMA programs have an obligation to determine whether the SMA is suitable for the investor client; this suitability obligation stems from the Advisers Act.

Rule 3a-4 does not specifically define suitability, but it is commonly thought to consist of at least the following five elements in the wrap fee context:

1. Is the portfolio manager suitable for the program?
2. Is the program suitable for the client?

---

[16] Stone, *supra* note 8, at 30–31.
[17] SEC 2008 CCOutreach Regional Seminars, "Top Deficiencies Identified," available at www.sec.gov/info/ccotopdeficiencies2008.pdf.

3. Is the chosen strategy suitable for the client?
4. Is the portfolio manager suitable for the client?
5. Are the portfolio manager's investments suitable for the client?[18]

Typically, the sponsor of the SMA program is responsible for determining the first four elements of the analysis immediately above, while each money manager is responsible for the fifth element.

In conjunction with its suitability obligation, the sponsor of an SMA program is typically responsible for completing some level of due diligence on the money managers included in an SMA program. According to Cerulli, "[t]he institutionalization of the manager selection process has been a development that has fueled the increased adoption of managed account programs over the last decade."[19] Cerulli attributed the broadening range of responsibilities for money manager analyst groups to "the seeming breakdown in adequate risk management and the heightened awareness of investment fraud" requiring analysts to seek more" transparency, requesting firm information more frequently and visiting managers more regularly."[20]

The most common factors analyzed by money manager analyst groups include (1) investment team expertise and manager tenure, (2) philosophy and process, (3) performance,[21] (4) impressions of key people, (5) risk controls, (6) style consistency, (7) volatility, and (8) fees.[22]

The money manager's fees are just one component of the traditional wrap fee. The other fee components typically include a clearing/custody fee, a sponsor fee, and an advisor-rep fee. These fee components and the resulting total fee are typically disclosed to the investor client through the sponsor's Schedule H to the Form ADV. The area of fee billing is an area of high concentration by regulators during an examination.

---

[18] Stone, *supra* note 8, at 12.
[19] Cerulli Associates, "The Cerulli Edge Managed Accounts" (2Q 2009).
[20] *Id.* at 2.
[21] "Wrap fee arrangements raise a number of issues relating to the presentation of portfolio manager performance. These issues include basic questions surrounding who 'owns' wrap account performance, responsibility for calculating performance and keeping records, and a range of specific methodological issues, including under the CFA Institute's Global Investment Performance Standards (GIPS)," Stone, *supra* note 8, at 25. See also *Clover Capital Management, Inc.* (SEC, October 28, 1986).
[22] Cerulli Associates, *supra* note 19, at 8.

ISSUES FOR THE FUTURE

The SMA industry has seen a significant growth in product offerings over the past 35 years. In addition to SMAs, the following types of products have developed:

- Mutual fund advisory programs[23]
- Registered representative as portfolio manager[24]
- Registered representative as advisor[25]
- Unified managed accounts[26]

As percentages of the entire managed account industry, these products account for the following portions of the industry,[27] as of December 31, 2008:

- SMA—36 percent
- Mutual fund advisory programs—28 percent
- Registered representative as portfolio manager—14 percent
- Registered representative as advisor—18 percent
- Unified managed accounts—4 percent

Unified managed accounts (UMAs) have been the primary focus of new product efforts in the industry over the past few years. However, challenges remain relating to the adoption of UMAs by advisors with respect to the

---

[23] The MMI defines a mutual fund advisory program as "[a] mutual fund program that allows investors to allocate their assets across multiple mutual funds. The program includes capabilities such as client profiling, fee-based pricing and rebalancing" (MMI Central, 2Q 2009).

[24] The MMI defines a rep-as-portfolio-manager program as "[a] fee-based, managed program that allows the financial services rep to act as portfolio manager" (MMI Central, 2Q 2009).

[25] The MMI defines a rep-as-advisor program as "[a] non-discretionary, fee-based, advisory program that enables an investor to hold different types of securities" (MMI Central, 2Q 2009).

[26] The MMI defines a unified managed account platform as, "[a] single account that houses multiple investment products such as SMAs, mutual funds and ETFs." A related concept, "unified managed household platform," is defined by the MMI to be "[a] placeholder that aggregates multiple accounts, supports the delivery of multiple products and provides the ability to manage an investor's portfolio in a comprehensive way" (MMI Central, 2Q 2009).

[27] Cerulli Online Roundtable, "Managed Accounts: Innovation and Competitive Dynamics in a Turbulent Market" (April 30, 2009).

amount of flexibility in the current generation of UMA products and the ability to implement fixed-income solutions within a UMA.[28]

Beyond the SMA industry's product development advancements, there has also been an increase in interest in SMAs outside the borders of the United States over the past 5 to 10 years. A number of SMA program sponsors now offer SMA programs in a variety of foreign jurisdictions. The establishment of these programs outside of the United States has proven challenging on several levels. First, the disparate regulatory structures in non-U.S. jurisdictions make it time-consuming and expensive to identify an SMA program structure that will work. Second, the sales process is just beginning in many of these foreign jurisdictions, making the often-encountered unfamiliarity with SMA products a significant hurdle. Third, the lack of familiarity of U.S. SMA sponsors with each jurisdiction's policies and procedures creates uncertainty among SMA program participants, such as money managers.

Notwithstanding the challenges, for many, a fee-based investment alternative with access to professional management not otherwise obtainable as an individual investor makes separately managed accounts an attractive investment option for both U. S. and non-U.S. investors.

---

[28] *Id.*

CHAPTER 13

International Compliance

THE FOUR HORSEMEN OF INTERNATIONAL COMPLIANCE

The following four items reflect the primary areas of concern for the international compliance departments of U.S. broker-dealers:

1. Foreign Exchange Controls
2. Laws of Inheritance
3. Tax Reporting
4. The U.S. Non-Resident Alien Transfer Tax

FOREIGN EXCHANGE CONTROLS

An exchange control is set by a national government and dictates how much money a resident may take out of his country or hold in a foreign currency. Controls may also limit who and how much may be invested in a country. The approach to exchange controls varies widely among countries. For example, some countries set a specific limit on outgoing money flows. Other countries require reporting of outgoing money and tax unreported money when it is brought back into the country. In a number of countries people may use securities transactions to avoid exchange controls and thus transfer money outside of the controls and established exchange rates. These controls are antithetical to global free trade ideals but, it must be noted, that in some countries such as India, for example, the strict exchange controls

allowed it to weather the economic turmoil in 2008 quite nicely because India was little affected by the collapse in Western markets.[1]

---

[1]The United States, through tax policy, influences global capital movements. For example, a 1963 tax levied on non-U.S. companies seeking to raise capital in the U.S. markets, effectively drove non-U.S. issuers seeking U.S. dollars to Europe (where dollars were accumulating as part of U.S. rebuilding aid to Europe after World War II)—precipitating the creation of the Eurobond market. The intended effect of the tax, of course, was to keep U.S. dollars in the United States. Conversely, the United States attracts deposits to U.S. banks by not imposing a withholding tax on the deposits of non-U.S. citizens.

TAX REPORTING

Closely related to exchange control violations is tax evasion. Not all countries have worldwide income taxation like the United States. Some countries only tax income earned within their own borders, which is why no-tax or low-tax jurisdictions such as the Cayman Islands, the Channel Islands, or Mauritius attract investors. However, many countries, including the United States, maintain that it is a criminal offense to not declare income earned abroad. A number of Latin American countries have "blacklisted" certain offshore tax havens, making it a presumptive criminal offense if their citizens are found to have undeclared accounts in those jurisdictions.[2]

LAWS OF INHERITANCE

Apart from an investor's desire for confidentiality and tax reduction provided by offshore jurisdictions, there are other attractions to establishing offshore holding companies and trusts. Many civil law jurisdictions have strict laws of inheritance—so-called *laws of succession*—that dictate who is entitled to inherit a decedent's property. Common law rules of inheritance (such as those in the BVI and the United States) generally allow a person to decide for himself who should inherit his property. Common law courts generally have not given effect to conflicting civil law rules of inheritance. This flexibility provides the creator of a common law trust with the opportunity to arrange for the transfer of assets after death in a manner contrary to that prescribed in the creator's country of residence.

NON-RESIDENT ALIEN ESTATE TAX

Another advantage of offshore accounts is that they can lawfully avoid the U.S. Non-Resident Alien Estate Tax if the accounts are established as offshore corporations. Currently, the estate of a nonresident individual who

---

[2]Tax evasion is a criminal offense in the United States and other jurisdictions as well. In some countries like Switzerland, tax evasion is not a crime. The Swiss draw a sharp distinction between tax fraud (a sheet submitted that says a person earned $100 when in fact he earned $1,000 would be tax fraud), which is illegal and tax evasion (failure to pay tax on hidden income), which is not.

owned more than $60,000 in U.S. situs assets can, generally speaking, be forced to file a U.S. Non-Resident Alien Estate Tax return and pay tax to the United States on the decedent's U.S. situs assets. An offshore corporate structure can lawfully avoid this tax since the U.S. situs assets are not considered to be owned by the decedent, which explains why so many sophisticated non-U.S. investors invest in the United States through offshore corporations or other personal investment vehicles in offshore jurisdictions. It should be noted that some foreign jurisdictions have estate tax treaties with the United States that largely eliminate this problem for residents of those countries.

COMPLIANCE CASE STUDY

Like water, money finds a way to flow despite efforts to impound it. While many think of suitcases of cash as the first way to move currency, consider the following case study, which uses securities trading as a method to avoid exchange controls.

Simon Bolivar

Venezuela

One of the tools used by compliance professionals when determining jurisdictional risk as it pertains to international compliance issues is the Corrupt

Perceptions Index (CPI), published annually by Transparency International. In 2001, Venezuela was listed in the bottom quartile of the 91 nations surveyed, falling into the bottom 23 percent. Since 2001, Venezuela has fallen further into the bottom tenth of an expanded list of nations, now totaling 180, moving downward to the 8 percent mark. This means that of all 180 jurisdictions surveyed in 2008, 92 percent of them are more transparent than Venezuela. This is an alarming trend from a compliance perspective.

At the same time that Venezuela was falling down the CPI ratings, negative press was mounting around items such as the terrorist financing of rebels in Colombia, the increased use of Venezuela as a drug trafficking transshipment point, increased levels of political corruption, and alliance-building with countries such as Iran.

Currency Controls   In 2003 Hugo Chavez implemented currency controls that restricted the flow of U.S. dollars into and out of Venezuela. The currency controls were purportedly implemented to stabilize the Venezuelan Bolivar and curb inflation. These currency controls require Venezuelan nationals and companies to obtain U.S. dollars only from a government entity named Comisión de Administración de Divisas (CADIVI), which is managed by the Venezuelan Ministry of Finance. CADIVI is tasked with regulating and restricting foreign currency exchange and exchange rates. U.S. dollars may only be sold to Venezuelan nationals or companies for limited purposes that include some import-export transactions, personal trips (limited to no more than U.S. $5,000 per annum), education abroad, and some medical reasons. As a result of the currency controls around U.S. dollars, a parallel unofficial exchange regime has arisen.

Permuta   The official exchange rate for bolivars to U.S. dollars is 2.15:1. This is the rate given through CADIVI, but is limited to certain transactions, and the associated paperwork to process this transaction is cumbersome and can take months to complete. The informal exchange rate or parallel exchange rate fluctuates around 6.5 to 7.0 bolivars per U.S. dollar. This is nearly 350 percent greater than the official exchange rate. The Venezuelan government has left open a door for the exchange of bolivars to U.S. dollars via a fairly complicated process that does not lend itself to transparency throughout the life cycle of the transaction. This process is called *permuta*, which means *a swap*.

If a Venezuelan national or company wants to move bolivars offshore in order to get USD, it must first deposit the bolivars in the bank account of a local broker-dealer (*casa de bolsa*) and then use those bolivars to purchase a bond denominated in bolivars. This part of the transaction is completed onshore in Venezuela.

The Bolivar-denominated bond is then transferred to an offshore entity typically incorporated in Panama, the Netherlands Antilles, the Cayman Islands, or the British Virgin Islands. This offshore company is typically set up by the onshore Venezuelan broker-dealer for its clients interested in *permuta* transactions. Once the Bolivar-denominated bond is received at the offshore entity, it is then swapped for a U.S. dollar-denominated bond held at a second offshore entity. The Bolivar-denominated bond is sent to the second offshore company and the U.S. dollar-denominated bond is sent to the client that initiated the transaction.

The second offshore entity is typically incorporated in an offshore jurisdiction and will likely have an account at a U.S. bank or broker-dealer. This second offshore entity then purchases the U.S. dollar-denominated bond from the initiating client at a predetermined price, and wires the proceeds of the transaction to that client's U.S. account. At the same time, the second offshore entity sells the Bolivar-denominated bond into the U.S. market.[3]

The transaction is diagrammed in Figure 13.1.

The entire process makes for a lawful avoidance of exchange controls but poses transparency challenges for the compliance officer. An additional issue arises when the second offshore company is conducting its activity in a U.S. account. If the sale of the U.S. dollar-denominated bonds is to

---

[3]Like Venezuela, Argentina maintains currency controls, which prevent Argentines from transferring dollars out of the country unless certain conditions are met. Similarly, an official exchange rate is maintained, which at times varies with the market rate. Conceptually like *permuta*, Argentines lawfully export money out of the country at market rates by using a process called *contado con liqui*. In this instance, in the simplest variation, Euroclear eligible debt is purchased locally by a customer in Argentina with pesos. The bond is then bought by an Argentine broker from his customer and sold in a riskless principal transaction by the Argentine broker to a U.S. counterpart for dollars. The dollars are then credited to the account of the customer, typically at a U.S. bank. The difference in purchase price and sale price by the customer builds in the market exchange rate. Though not prohibited by the Comisión Nacional de Valores, these types of transactions warrant further scrutiny to determine that some market risk is borne in the transaction. This ensures that the process is not a complete method of exchange-control avoidance.

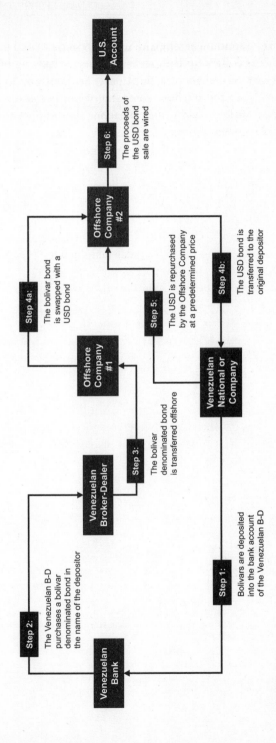

FIGURE 13.1 A Permuta Transaction

The following labels appear within the figure:

- U.S. Account
- Step 6: The proceeds of the USD bond sale are wired
- Offshore Company #2
- Step 4a: The bolivar bond is swapped with a USD bond
- Step 5: The USD is repurchased by the Offshore Company at a predetermined price
- Step 4b: The USD bond is transferred to the original depositor
- Offshore Company #1
- Venezuelan National or Company
- Venezuelan Broker-Dealer
- Step 3: The bolivar denominated bond is transferred offshore
- Step 2: The Venezuelan B-D purchases a bolivar denominated bond in the name of the depositor
- Step 1: Bolivars are deposited into the bank account of the Venezuelan B-D
- Venezuelan Bank

effect a *permuta* transaction whereby a U.S. dollar-denominated instrument is converted into U.S. dollars for the express purpose of moving funds from one place to another on behalf of a third party without any market risk to the participants, then the offshore company, if not licensed in the U.S. to provide money transfer services, may be acting as an unlicensed money transmitter under U.S. regulations.

CHAPTER 14

Money Laundering

Money laundering, in a simple memorable phrase, is "doing sneaky things with dirty money." The criminal, with ill-gotten gains from selling drugs or racketeering, disguises his ownership of these proceeds of crime in a series of obfuscating transactions using accounts whose true ownership is not known in which he places a series of transactions that are difficult to trace.[1]

In the 1960s in the United States, a number of forces converged that put money laundering into focus. The cost of the Vietnam War, coupled with the cost of funding President Lyndon Johnson's social reforms, drove the need for new tax revenues. Thus, the requirement for banks to report large cash transactions was born out of an attempt by tax authorities to learn of large sources of cash deposits. The idea was to ferret out large sources of cash under the assumption that the depositors were criminals who had not paid tax on their drug profits or racketeering proceeds. See 31 U.S.C. §§ 5311–5332 (now known as the Bank Secrecy Act).

Congress upped the ante in 1986 in President Reagan's war on drugs by criminalizing money laundering. See 18 U.S.C. §§ 1956, 1957.

The terrorist attacks on the World Trade Center and Pentagon on September 11, 2001, precipitated another change in the obligations of financial companies to detect and prevent money laundering and terrorist financing. By October, Congress passed and the President signed the sweeping legislation known as the USA PATRIOT Act.[2]

---

[1]The International Monetary Fund estimates that between $500 billion and $1.5 trillion a year is laundered through the world's financial system. "Money Laundering," *The Economist*, April 14, 2001, at 64. Somewhere between one-third and one-half of that amount enters the United States as laundered funds. "Private Banking: RIP," *Forbes*, November 12, 2001, at 80.

[2]"Uniting and Strengthening America by Providing Appropriate Tools Required to Intercept and Obstruct Terrorism Act of 2001" (USA PATRIOT Act), Pub. L. No. 107–56, 115 Stat.

The immediate effect was that offshore entities and individuals were subject to significantly more scrutiny by U.S. financial institutions (e.g., U.S. financial institutions now demand to know the identities of settlors and beneficiaries of trusts). Limited liability companies were forced by U.S. institutions to give up the names of members and managers and closely held corporations, and were forced to reveal their beneficial owners. The Anti-Money Laundering Best Practices, published by the Securities Industry and Financial Markets Association, is illustrative of these new best practices. These can be found at www.sifma.com.

Prior to September 11, 2001, the United States had been somewhat solicitous to investors, especially foreign investors, and their perceived needs for privacy. For example, the IRS's Qualified Intermediary Program (QI Program) balanced privacy concerns with the demands of the U.S. tax system. In light of September 11, 2001, some have suggested that some provisions of the USA PATRIOT Act are now in direct conflict with the QI Program.[3]

Prior to September 11, 2001, the NYSE was also somewhat sympathetic to privacy arguments. For example, the NYSE supported the right of foreign fiduciaries not to have to disclose the names of their customers to U.S. institutions, recognizing that their home country's laws or normative codes might prevent them from doing so. The NYSE also recognized that forcing foreign fiduciaries to disclose the names of their customers would put the U.S. markets at a competitive disadvantage.[4] These concerns now fall on deaf ears.

The September 11 terrorist attacks were the good and immediate reasons for the USA PATRIOT Act. However, several components of the legislation had been circulating in Congress long before September 11, 2001, primarily as a result of scandals in U.S. private and correspondent banking.[5]

The reality is that much larger geopolitical issues are embedded in the USA PATRIOT Act than the United States' current war on terrorism.

272 (codified as amended in scattered sections of U.S.C.A.; providing enhanced government powers in a number of areas including electronic surveillance, immigration, and anti-money laundering).
[3]Carol P. Tello, Esq., "Potential Tax Implications of the Enhanced Money Laundering Provisions of USA PATRIOT ACT," *Daily Tax Report*, November 5, 2001.
[4]Exchange Act Release No. 13388 (March 18, 1977); see also Exchange Act Release No. 13149 (January 10, 1977).
[5]Senate Permanent Subcommittee on Investigations, "Correspondent Banking A Gateway to Money Laundering" (February 2001); "Private Banking and Money Laundering: A Case Study of Opportunities and Vulnerabilities," S.Hrg. 106–428 (November 9 and 10, 1999).

The USA PATRIOT Act embodies measures directed at rooting out tax evasion by U.S. and foreign citizens, exposing the kleptocrats of foreign nations, and ferreting out the drug dealers and racketeers.[6] For example, Section 315 of the USA PATRIOT Act expands the list of foreign crimes that are now considered specific unlawful activity (SUA) when they involve a financial transaction occurring in whole or in part in the United States. This activity now exposes greater numbers of financial consultants, lawyers, bankers, and accountants to potential prosecution under U.S. money laundering laws. New types of SUA include crimes of violence, smuggling, or export control violations relating to certain munitions, bribery of a foreign public official, misappropriation or embezzlement of foreign public funds, and any offense with respect to which the United States is obligated by a multilateral treaty to extradite or prosecute the offender.[7]

The potential impact of the expansive new scope of U.S. money-laundering laws is further amplified by new tax information agreements entered into by the United States.

The Organisation for Economic Co-operation and Development has been for years pressuring so-called *tax haven countries* to become more transparent and cooperate better with overseas tax and criminal investigations. Countries that fail to cooperate risk being "named and shamed" by the Financial Action Task Force (FATF).[8] The practical effect of this publicity is that institutions are going to give heightened scrutiny to any account located in these noncooperative jurisdictions because regulators will view any account located there as a "red flag," because tax evaders and worse are known to move money to these jurisdictions.[9]

---

[6]The convergence of social forces precipitating changes in financial regulation is nothing new. The first major piece of U.S. legislation passed in 1970 is familiar to all by its requirements for U.S. financial institutions to file Currency Transactions Reports. Bank Secrecy Act, 31 U.S.C. § 5311 (1970). It was designed to enable law enforcement to collect data on those engaged in cash transactions in an effort to both collect more tax and stop illegal cash businesses.

[7]What this means at a practical level is that a broker or investment advisor must "know the customer." Like facets on a diamond, there are many faces to a customer: a credit component (can the client pay for the securities?), an identity component (is this person who he says he is?), a suitability component (is there enough information about the client for the broker or advisor to recommend the right investment?), and a source and use of funds component (where does the money come from and where is it going?). All of this should be verified, preferably through independent channels. As Vladimir Lenin said, "Trust, but verify." In Russian, the phrase is more memorable since it rhymes—"Doveryai, no Proveryai."

[8]FATF was formed by the G-7 nations in 1989 and now has many members from the world's major industrialized nations.

[9]See William F. Wechsler, "Follow the Money," 80 *Foreign Affairs* 40 (Summer 2001).

The USA PATRIOT Act has continuing impact. It contains many provisions directed at offshore entities doing business with U.S. institutions, including provisions related to preventing U.S. institutions from doing business with shell banks (§ 313); "special due diligence" for correspondent and private banking customers, including identification of beneficial owners (§ 312); account opening identification and verification standards (§ 326); special measures for institutions, countries or transactions of primary money laundering concern (§ 311); and new regulations for concentration and omnibus accounts (§ 325).

To be sure, the privacy concerns so prominent in the Gramm-Leach-Bliley legislation, passed in 1999, have taken a back seat. Specifically, Section 314 of the USA PATRIOT Act provides that none of the privacy provisions of Gramm-Leach-Bliley shall stand in the way of compliance with the USA PATRIOT Act. Moreover, Section 314 calls on financial institutions to share financial information with each other when they have suspicions of money laundering or terrorist financing.

In the EU, the Commission has implemented a series of Money Laundering Directives to provide a common legal basis across the EU for the prevention and sanction of money-laundering activities. The EU has formulated its Directives to implement the recommendations of the FATF and ensure that anti-money laundering efforts are consistent with the EU.

The first Money Laundering Directive (2001) concentrated on combating the laundering of drug proceeds through the traditional financial sector. This imposed obligations on firms within the financial sector to maintain adequate systems for customer identification, staff training, record keeping, and reporting of suspicious transactions. The second Money Laundering Directive (2001) expanded the scope of the first by expanding the types of offenses for which suspicious transaction reporting was mandatory, from drug trafficking to all serious offenses, and extended the Directive's scope to nonfinancial activities and professions (including lawyers, notaries, accountants, estate agents, art dealers, jewelers, auctioneers, and casinos). The third Money Laundering Directive (2005/60/EC) reflects the FATF's 2003 Recommendations (thereby updating and replacing the first and second Directives accordingly), which further extended the scope of the provisions to cover the financing of terrorism as well as money laundering.

The EU Directives have been implemented in the United Kingdom primarily through the Counter Terrorism Act 2008, the Money Laundering Regulations 2007, the Proceeds of Crime Act 2002 (as amended by the

Serious Organised Crime and Police Act 2005), and the Terrorism Act 2000 (as amended by the Anti-Terrorism, Crime and Security Act 2001). Pursuant to the U.K. legislation, credit institutions, financial institutions, auditors, accountants, tax advisors, legal professionals, estate agents, and certain other institutions at risk from money-laundering activity are required to put in place certain controls, which include assessments of the risk to their business of money-laundering activity, checks on the identity of their customers with appropriate due diligence measures (which may be more or less stringent depending on the risk profile of the customer), checks on the identity of "beneficial owners" of corporate bodies and partnerships, monitoring of customers' business activities and reporting anything suspicious to the Serious Organized Crime Agency (SOCA), implementation of staff training, and keeping appropriate documentary evidence of the above. Firms are also required to appoint a dedicated money laundering reporting officer (MLRO) to review information, monitor compliance with the regulations and report any suspicious activity to the SOCA. Failure to comply with the provisions of the U.K. money-laundering legislation constitutes a criminal offense, punishable by imprisonment and/or a fine. Good practice guidance and practical assistance in interpreting the U.K. money-laundering legislation for the financial services industry is provided by the Joint Money Laundering Steering Group Guidelines (available at www.jmlsg.org.uk).

On a broader level, the fight against money laundering and terrorist financing is led by the leadership of the FATF, which is based in Paris. Much in the same way that the Bank of International Settlements influences capital adequacy standards for banks internationally, FATF helps shape anti-money laundering guidelines internationally.

ANTI-MONEY LAUNDERING CASE STUDY

Ever-changing regulation creates new challenges for risk, compliance, and legal officers at banks and broker dealers. However, one theme is constant. Whether in need of revenues to support welfare states or develop economies, nations chase people who are believed to be evading taxes. The illustration that follows concerning Argentina is one of many examples of the theme and the further discussion of "blue money" and *United States v. Pasquantino* highlights the potential pitfalls for those who knowingly assist tax evasion.

Argentina

Argentine nationals are subject to an income tax as well as a global holdings tax and, for a variety of reasons, many Argentineans maintain accounts outside of Argentina. In December 2008, Argentina declared a tax amnesty that does not require disclosure of the provenance of funds being repatriated from offshore holdings. This program was intended to help stimulate the Argentine economy.

In May 2009, the Banco Central de la República Argentina (BCRA) issued a new resolution that prohibited companies incorporated in, or individuals domiciled in, or a resident of, a blacklisted jurisdiction from trading in the Argentine securities market. Argentine nationals are also prohibited from transferring assets directly to a blacklisted jurisdiction. Jurisdictions blacklisted by Argentina are typically tax haven countries or countries that have not entered into an exchange of information and cooperation agreement with Argentina. This new resolution has left offshore entities

Eva Peron

searching for a new access point to the Argentine markets, and has left on-shore financial institutions in Argentina searching for new methods to safely move assets offshore to the blacklisted jurisdictions.

White Money, Blue Money, and Black Money   Compliance officers have an argot to describe the different sources for money that moves through the financial system. "White Money" is those funds that are legitimately earned and are fully reported to all appropriate governments for tax purposes. These funds move through traditional financial networks, such as banks, regulated casas de cambio, broker-dealers, and other registered and licensed financial institutions. The movement of these funds is fully transparent, and includes the name of the originator and/or beneficiary (e.g., the true owner of the funds being transferred). These money movements are also recorded and subject to review by the regulator(s) responsible for examining the financial institution.

"Blue Money" is those funds that are legitimately earned, but are *not* reported to all of the appropriate governments for tax purposes. These funds move through unlicensed and unregulated intermediary accounts set up by or for a local casa de cambio, casa de bolsa, travel agency, or other financial institution or entity. These intermediary accounts are typically shell companies set up outside of Argentina that are not subject to the review of a regulator. These intermediary entities typically do not maintain asset transfer records beyond the life of the transaction. Blue Money moved through these intermediaries is sent on- or offshore to or from Argentina in the name of the intermediary and not the true owner of the funds. Taxation authorities are not able to link the intermediary fund movements to the true owner of the funds.

"Black Money" is those funds not legitimately earned, and then not reported for taxation purposes. These funds move through the same channels as Blue Money, making it difficult for compliance staffs to distinguish the two types of funds, particularly when third-party intermediaries are involved.

United States v. Pasquantino   A U.S. financial firm could run afoul of U.S. law if it knowingly assists Argentinean nationals to evade taxes through the knowing facilitation of intermediary transfers. In 2005 the U.S. Supreme Court decided a case called *United States v. Pasquantino* that established that a plot to defraud a foreign government of tax revenues (in this case, Canadian customs duties on alcohol) that has a U.S. nexus (use of the

Samples of stamps reflecting taxes paid.

telephone in the United States) is a federal crime. The ruling overturned established law that one country would not look to enforce the tax laws of another country. As a result of this case, financial firms that knowingly directly or indirectly assist a client with hiding funds from non-U.S. tax authorities may be committing a federal crime.

CHAPTER 15

SIPC and Other Investment Protection Schemes around the World

In the United States, if a broker-dealer were to become insolvent, any bankruptcy proceeding would be governed by the Security Investor Protection Act (SIPA), which incorporates by reference much of the U.S. Bankruptcy Code. SIPA and the U.S. Bankruptcy Code essentially separate the insolvent broker-dealer's estate into three parts—"customer name securities," "customer property," and the remaining assets. SIPA generally bestows priority on the claims of a "customer" over a broker-dealer's unsecured creditors with respect to customer name securities and customer property.[1]

Section 16(4) of SIPA defines the term *customer property* to include "cash and securities (except customer name securities delivered to the customer) at any time received, acquired, or held by or for the account of a debtor from or for the securities accounts of a customer, and the proceeds of

---

[1]Section 16(2) of SIPA defines the term *customer* of a debtor (i.e., the broker-dealer) to include "any person (including any person with whom the debtor deals as principal or agent) who has a claim on account of securities received, acquired, or held by the debtor in the ordinary course of its business as a broker or dealer from or for the securities accounts of such person for safekeeping, with a view to sale, to cover consummated sales, pursuant to purchases, as collateral security, or for purposes of effecting transfer." Section 16(3) of SIPA defines the term *customer name securities* to include securities "held for the account of a customer on the filing date by or on behalf of the debtor and which on the filing date were registered in the name of the customer, or were in the process of being so registered pursuant to instructions from the debtor." Customer name securities generally are returned to their respective customers. However, if the customer owes money to the broker-dealer, then the customer must satisfy that debt and obtain the approval of the bankruptcy trustee before reclaiming the customer name securities.

any such property transferred by the debtor, including property unlawfully converted." Customer property is returned to each customer based on the customer's net equity, which is determined by adding (1) the amount of cash held in the customer's account to (2) the value of securities held in such account (determined as of the SIPA filing date), and subtracting (3) any amounts the customer owes to the broker-dealer.

PROTECTION OF CUSTOMER ASSETS BY SIPC AND EXCESS SIPC COVERAGE

If the distribution of customer name securities and customer property from the broker-dealer does not satisfy a customer's overall net equity claim, the Securities Investor Protection Corporation (SIPC), which administers SIPA, provides protection of up to $500,000 per customer, except that only $100,000 of the SIPC protection can be applied toward a loss of a cash balance carried in an account at an insolvent broker-dealer. If a customer's net equity claim remains unsatisfied after the distribution of customer name securities and customer property and the payment of the SIPC funds, the customer becomes an unsecured creditor and will be paid out of any remaining assets of the broker-dealer's estate. A broker-dealer may obtain private insurance to cover customer losses in excess of the amounts paid. This private insurance is referred to as *excess SIPC* and applies to assets held in custody at the broker-dealer, subject to contractually imposed limits.

REGULATORY OBLIGATIONS ON CUSTODY OF CUSTOMER FUNDS AND SECURITIES

Under normal circumstances, regulatory obligations of a broker-dealer holding customer funds and securities should obviate the need to rely on SIPC protection or excess SIPC coverage to satisfy customers' claims in a bankruptcy proceeding. In particular, the need to rely on SIPC protection and excess SIPC coverage should arise only in the unlikely event that a broker-dealer had not segregated sufficient customer funds and securities pursuant to the SEC's Customer Protection Rule, Rule 15c3-3 under the 1934 Act. In particular, the Customer Protection Rule requires a broker-dealer to segregate customers' funds in a separate bank account and to maintain possession or control of customers' fully paid and excess margin securities.[2] The correspondent firms' customers are considered a clearing broker's customers for purposes of the Customer Protection Rule.[3]

With respect to customer funds, the Customer Protection Rule requires a broker-dealer to make a periodic computation (generally every Friday), according to a specified formula (Reserve Formula), to determine the amount of funds that it must have on deposit in a special reserve bank account for the exclusive benefit of customers (Special Reserve Account). Under the Reserve Formula, a broker-dealer is required to determine how much money it is holding that is either customer money or money obtained from the use of customer securities (Credits). From that figure, the broker-dealer is required to subtract the amount of money that it is owed by customers or by other broker-dealers relating to customer transactions (Debits). If the Debits exceed the Credits, no deposit to the Special Reserve Account is necessary. However, if the Credits exceed the Debits, the broker-dealer is required to deposit the excess amount (generally by the following Tuesday) into the Special Reserve Account. In addition, the broker-dealer may not withdraw funds from the Special Reserve Account until it completes a computation that shows that it has on deposit more funds than the Reserve Formula requires.

With respect to customer securities, the Customer Protection Rule requires a broker-dealer to promptly obtain and thereafter maintain physical possession or control of all fully paid and excess margin securities carried by the broker-dealer for the account of customers. In effect, the Customer Protection Rule requires the broker-dealer to segregate fully paid and excess margin securities from its proprietary securities and to make a daily determination that it has sufficient securities segregated. If the broker-dealer determines on a given day that it has fewer securities in its possession or control than is required, the broker-dealer is required to eliminate the deficit within specified time frames, generally within one or two days. In order to be considered to have possession or control of customer securities, the broker-dealer must hold the securities in an account in its name at a central clearing corporation or depository, free of any lien, or at a bank supervised by a federal banking authority, free of any lien.

The operation of the U.S. Customer Protection Rule is somewhat in contrast to the corresponding regulatory scheme in the United Kingdom. While the custody and client money rules of the U.K.'s Financial Services Authority

---

[2] *Excess margin* securities are securities held in a customer's margin account whose value exceeds 140 percent of the margin loans extended to the customer.

[3] Rule 15c3-3(a)(1) defines the term *customer* to include "any person from whom or on whose behalf a broker or dealer has received or acquired or holds funds or securities for the account of that person." Securities Exchange Act of 1934, 15 U.S.C. §§ 78(a) et seq. (1934).

The French investment in Panama, like the Scots' investment before them, ended disastrously.

provide protections similar to those of the Customer Protection Rule, the U.K. rules allow institutional customers to effectively opt out of those rules in certain circumstances. In particular, a U.K. broker-dealer may enter into a "title transfer collateral arrangement" with a customer, under which the customer transfers full ownership of securities and money to the broker-dealer for the purposes of securing or otherwise covering present or future, actual or contingent or prospective obligations. The customer then has no proprietary claim to the securities and money transferred, and would rank only as a general creditor of the broker-dealer with respect to any claim for the payment of the securities and money, which may be irrecoverable in the event of any insolvency or default. Where a U.K. broker-dealer typically enters into title transfer arrangements with clients, it appears that, in practice, the U.K. broker-dealer may charge higher rates and fees for margin and other services to institutional customers that wish to have their funds and securities covered by the custody and client money rules. The insolvency of Lehman Brothers International in London has brought these issues to the fore.

Japan, Taiwan, Canada, Australia, and South Korea also provide investor protection insurance. An EU Directive passed in 1997, the Investor Protection Directive, dictates an investor protection coverage of at least 20,000 euros. National legislation that implements the directive in the various European nations is still being developed.

CHAPTER 16

Risk Management

Any number of risks can be associated with trading in the international securities markets and we have already covered many of them throughout the course of the book. In order to clarify one's thinking on the topic, a short taxonomy is provided below. Each individual risk is beyond the scope of this book; each could be the subject of an entire book. Given its topicality, Value at Risk (VaR) is examined because it is not widely understood and its use as a risk measurement has been blamed, in part, for the 2008 recession.

Credit risk is the risk that a counterparty will not settle a transaction. This can be the customer side of a transaction or the market side as a result of a market counterparty failing to settle a trade (*settlement risk*).

Market risk is the risk associated with an adverse movement in the price of the asset.

Legal risk is the risk associated with the inability to enforce a contract due to a documentation failure or due to conducting an unauthorized business that renders a lawful contract unenforceable.

Operational risk is the risk associated with a deficiency in internal procedures.

Custody risk is the risk associated with the insolvency of a custodian or cash or the occurrence of other circumstances preventing the custodian from delivering securities or cash on request.

Credit risk, of course, is mitigated in a variety of subtle and simple ways. Margin requirements, good-faith deposits, guarantees, indemnification rights, liens, and rights of set-off are all part of the risk-mitigation techniques. Part and parcel of credit risk management is making sure on the legal side that such credit risk mitigants, such as guarantees and liens, are legally enforceable. We have already covered in this book risks associated with custody risk and settlement risk. This leaves market risk and its interplay with credit risk for further discussion.

In the 1990s, a number of banks and brokerages began to use a risk paradigm known as Value at Risk (VaR). At its simplest, VaR attempts to measure future risk of a portfolio of financial assets moving one way or another based on observed trends from the past.[1] Typically, VaR is used to assess the risk of a firm's proprietary holdings, but it can be used as a measurement in evaluating whether to extend credit as well. As Professor Philippe Jorion in his seminal work *Value at Risk* describes it: "VaR summarizes the worst loss over a target horizon that will not be exceeded with a given confidence level." Here is how it works at its most basic.

Over a defined period of time, the variation of the price of a security is ascertained (say, for example, the daily movement of an equity price over the past three years). Assume 252 trading days a year. There may be only seven days where the stock in question dropped more than $3 on any given day in the 756-day period.

The variations can be plotted on a graph (and assuming a normal distribution) with the less frequent major price movements reflected in the "tails" of the curve. See Figure 16.1.

Last, to complete the VaR analysis, a "confidence level" is applied, meaning at what value point, say one percent of the time (the standard for risk managers), there will be a loss. It is that value that forms the VaR. If the portfolio consisted of 100 shares of one security with a total value of $1,000, the VaR would be $3 in this example because one percent of the time (7 out of 756) the stock dips more than $3. Stated another way, 99 percent of the time the portfolio would not lose more than $3 per day.

The reader is referred to the books cited in footnote 1 for a more in-depth explanation.

As stated above, VaR is just one tool for the risk manager. Of equal importance are security concentrations in the portfolio (whether by security or sector) and the liquidity of the securities that make up the portfolio. For

---

[1]See Kenneth L. Grant, *Trading Risk: Enhanced Profitability Through Risk Control* (John Wiley & Sons 2004); Philippe Jorion, *Value at Risk: The New Benchmark for Managing Financial Risk* (McGraw-Hill 2006); Nassim Taleb, *The Black Swan: The Impact of the Highly Improbable* (Random House 2007).

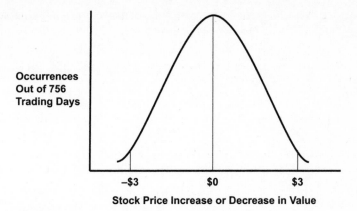

Occurrences Out of 756 Trading Days

−$3 $0 $3

Stock Price Increase or Decrease in Value

FIGURE 16.1   A Simple VaR Graphic

example, a lender might require that no portfolio against which credit is extended contain more than 5 percent of any one issue of securities or more than 20 percent of any one sector of the securities market. As a practical example as it relates to security liquidity, a rule of thumb a lender might follow is that if the number of shares held in an account for a unique security is greater than three days' trading volume, then the firm will not finance inventory or a customer's position beyond that amount, absent a guarantee or some other form of collateral. Recent market events have proven that in times of distress, it becomes difficult to solicit bids for illiquid positions, and generally investors end up "chasing the market," causing an accelerated decline in the price of the collateral. Therefore, a liquidity cap is another good item in the risk manager's toolkit.

Conclusion

International investing poses challenges like none other. Of course, that is what makes it exciting for investors and market professionals alike. The most recent financial panic in 2008 has brought about a renewed call for international cooperation across securities markets. Just as the EU has set forth on a determined course to unify its securities markets, it is logical that other regions like the Middle East and Asia will follow. However, as long as there are national borders and as long as national regulators retain powers not superseded by a supranational body, cross-border challenges will remain and will need to be understood. Hopefully, this book has helped.

If this book has succeeded[1] in its mission, the reader is in a better position after reading it to understand the international markets and the associated challenges of executing, clearing, and safekeeping securities in those markets.

---

[1]What is success? In a quote often misattributed to Ralph Waldo Emerson (but actually by Bessie A. Stanley), "he has achieved success who has lived well, laughed often, and loved much; . . . [and enjoyed] the respect of intelligent men and the love of little children. . . ." Joseph Mitchell Chapple, ed., *Heart Throbs, Vol. II*, Boston: Chapple Publishing Co., 1911. p. 1–2. With respect to the respect of intelligent men and women, constructive criticism of this book is welcomed at george.arnett3@gmail.com

Afterword

As an investment professional, you are no doubt aware that information is knowledge, and that knowledge can be power. Fortunately, as you have discovered, you hold in your hands one of the most informative, comprehensive, and valuable guides to the complex and interconnected world of global securities markets.

Increasingly, however, information alone is not enough to enable financial services professionals to gain the understanding necessary to take effective action and to do what is right for their clients or their firms. What is needed is context, and the ability to turn ideas into action. And it is here that my colleague George (Tres) Arnett provides us all with perhaps his most valuable contribution to the library of understanding surrounding the global securities market. In page after page, and chapter after chapter, his depth of understanding and ability to see how the pieces work together take the reader beyond simple facts to true comprehension.

Running throughout this important and exciting work, however, is the knowledge that for all of the opportunity represented in the world's securities markets, there are other equally critical components that must be understood: namely, the legal precepts that bind markets together and the buyers and sellers who are their lifeblood. It is this context—that our globalized financial markets can only function successfully if the regulatory schemes that govern their behavior are adhered to and understood—that may prove to be the most valuable aspect of this book.

In short, you could ask for no better place than the outstanding work between these covers to begin or continue on your journey through the exciting world of global securities markets. Hopefully, Tres's lasting contribution to the body of knowledge governing global markets will be found in the increased number of financial professionals who are able to move from reading the facts to truly understanding and taking the right actions in service to themselves, their customers, and the industry in which they operate.

HUGH JONES IV

Hugh Jones is president and CEO of Accuity and NRS, two companies that lead their markets by providing compliance solutions to the financial services industry. Additional information and best practices applications related to some of the material in this book, in particular Chapter 6 regarding the regulatory framework and Chapter 14 regarding "Know Your Customer" practices, can be found at www.accuitysolutions.com/GSM

Glossary

best execution   The obligation of a broker to find the best price for his customer given the time of the order, the size of the order, and a variety of other factors.

bilateral contracts   An agreement between two parties in which both parties exchange reciprocal promises.

Blue Sky   The Blue Sky Laws are the regulatory framework created by the individual states that make up the United States. Thus, there are two tiers of regulation in the United States: a federal level and a state level.

central counterparty   Acts as the seller to every buyer and the buyer to every seller to negate the risk that one party becomes insolvent before netting or settlement takes place.

collateralized debt obligation   A financial instrument whose value is correlated to a portfolio of fixed income assets, such as bonds and loans.

credit risk   The risk a counterparty will not settle a transaction. This can be the customer side of a transaction or the market side as a result of a market counterparty failing to settle a trade.

custodian   Financial institution that is responsible for the record keeping and servicing of customer assets, typically a bank or broker.

custody risk   Risk associated with the insolvency of a custodian of securities or cash or the occurrence of other circumstances preventing the custodian from delivering securities or cash on request.

debentures   A debt security that has only a corporation's future profits as security for future payment.

dematerialized   Not in physical form due to automation and the development of Central Securities Depositories, securities have moved away from physical form to being traded electronically.

derivative   A financial instrument directly correlated to an underlying equity, bond, or other product. Derivatives can be used to insure against risk (hedge) or to acquire risk (speculate).

discretion   An investor may give over to her broker investment-making decision power. In that situation, the broker has discretion to make suitable trades for the investor without the investor approving each trade.

entitlement holder   Person noted in bank's or broker's records as the owner of securities.

EU Directives   EU Directives are European guidelines for regulation of securities and financial institutions and contain measures providing for investor protection. EU Directives have provisions for capital requirements, fair disclosure to investors, and measures intended to reduce barriers to entry in the marketplace and promote efficient price discovery. Directives must be implemented by each EU state.

forward   Right to purchase a foreign exchange asset in the future at an agreed-on price and time.

fund of hedge funds   A fund of hedge funds is an investment vehicle that aggregates the performance of several underlying hedge funds. The investors incur profits/losses in proportion to their holdings and the earnings of the underlying hedge funds.

fungible   Interchangeable.

future   Right to purchase any security or asset at a set price and time at a future date.

hedge fund   A hedge fund is a private investment vehicle. A hedge fund pools investor's money and often employs leverage, arbitrage, and long-short trading strategies to maximize returns for investors. Hedge funds typically collect a 2 percent management fee (based on client assets) as well as 20 percent of the earnings of the fund if the fund reaches or surpasses an established return level.

hypothecation   Used to mean either the pledge or loan of securities.

immobilize   To "freeze" in one place. Immobilization is one of the key functions of a Central Securities Depository. It allows for easy and efficient transfer of securities between brokers in one centralized location.

indenture trustee   Typically the corporate trust department of a bank. An indenture trustee collects the issuer's bond interest payments and pays them to the bondholder.

intermediated holdings   A bank or brokerage house is a typical intermediary. An intermediary stands between the investor and the issuer of securities.

legal risk   Risk associated with the inability to enforce a contract due to documentation failure or due to conducting an unauthorized business, which renders a lawful contract unenforceable.

leverage   Leverage refers to the borrowing of money to support securities trading. Leverage is used in retail brokerage accounts by utilizing a margin loan. From an investment perspective, leverage can magnify returns, but can also amplify losses.

margin loan   Borrowed money used to purchase securities.

market manipulation   Market abuses such as insider trading and other deceptive trading practices such as matched orders and wash sales.

market risk   The risk associated with an adverse movement in the price of an asset.

MiFID   MiFID (Markets in Financial Instruments Directive) rules for the best execution of transactions in a broad-reaching EU Directive. MiFID contains reporting obligations, and the assessment of suitability and appropriateness of investments for investors.

multiplier effect   Money in a box under a bed or gold in a strong box is not in use. Money invested or money lent, like a pebble in a pond, ripples throughout the economy because the borrower buys goods and services with it. The effect on the economy is known as the multiplier effect.

offshore account   A type of account held outside of the country of domicile, typically used to deposit funds in no-tax or low-tax jurisdiction. Offshore accounts can be for asset protection, privacy, or any number of legitimate reasons.

operational risk   Risk associated with a deficiency in internal procedures.

option   Type of derivative instrument whose value is based on the value of the underlying security and is defined by the underlying security's volatility.

preferred shares   A class of stock senior to common stock but junior to bonds commonly reflected on customer statements as a fixed income security. Preferred shares typically pay a set dividend and trade like fixed income securities.

private equity funds   Private equity funds are pooled investments that invest in various public and private companies. The companies that the private equity funds invest in are called *portfolio* companies and are typically managed with the insight and oversight of the private equity fund.

private placements   Private placements are securities not traded in the open market that are issued by corporations to a select set of investors. Private placements are often purchased by institutional investors or otherwise qualified purchasers.

prospectus   A legal document that provides details that an investor needs to make an informed decision.

proxy statements   Used by public companies to allow shareholders to make informed decisions about corporate events at shareholder meetings.

real estate funds   A real estate fund is a pool of investments that allows investors to gain broad exposure to the real estate market through the fund's investment in property or in corporations whose business involves property investment.

root of title   The way in which a person establishes a formal, legal link to ownership of a security.

Securities Act of 1933   Governs the issuance of new securities through mandating the disclosure or important financial information.

separately managed account   A type of investment account authorized by Rule 3(a)4 of the Investment Company Act, which provides for a sponsor to administer the account and for a third-party money manager to manage the client assets in a particular investment management style for a single asset-based fee.

Securities Exchange Act of 1934 Governs the securities markets and their participants through the creation of the Securities and Exchange Commission (SEC) and mandating ongoing disclosure of financial information.

stock power Physical piece of paper typically attached to the physical stock certificate used to legally transfer ownership of the certificate from one person to another.

suitability That an investment strategy meets the objectives and means of an investor, financial professionals have a duty to take steps that ensure that an investment is appropriate for a client.

swaps Type of derivative instrument that allows exchanging fixed-rate assets to variable-rate assets across currency or other types of assets.

transfer agent Hired by an issuer of securities to keep an accurate log of the owners of a company's securities.

U.S. situs assets Assets located within the United States.

unified managed account A type of investment account that houses multiple investment management styles and multiple investment types (such as ETFs and mutual funds) in a single account for a single asset-based fee.

value at risk A single measurement of a portfolios risk based on historic trading data.

warrants Often sold in units along with common stock, warrants allow the holder to buy stock from the issuing company at a preestablished price. Units are often separated after issuance and warrants may trade separately from the associated common stock.

wire house Large institutional firm that couples investment banking with a large distribution network of brokers. The term originates from the private network of telephone lines the firm once employed allowing bankers and brokers to stay connected across the United States.

wrap fee program Allows end client to pay one bundled fee for an advisory service rather than fees for brokerage commissions, investment advice, and other fees.

Further Reading

Adams Jr., Charles Francis, and Henry Adams. *Chapters of Erie*. Ithaca, New York: Cornell University Press, 1968.

Ahamed, Liaquat. *Lords of Finance: The Bankers Who Broke the World*. New York: Penguin Press, 2009.

Atack, Jeremy, and Larry Neal. *The Origin and Development of Financial Markets and Institutions: From the Seventeenth Century to the Present*. Cambridge University Press, 2009.

Balen, Malcolm. *The Secret History of the South Sea Bubble: The World's First Great Financial Scandal*. Cambridge, London: Fourth Estate, 2002.

Board of Governors of the Federal Reserve System. *The Federal Reserve System: Purposes & Functions*. Washington D.C., Publication Services, 1984.

Bookstaber, Richard. *A Demon of Our Own Design: Markets, Hedge Funds, and the Perils of Financial Innovation*. Hoboken, NJ: John Wiley & Sons, 2007.

Brooks, John. *The GoGo Years: The Drama and Crashing Finale of Wall Street's Bullish 60s*. New York: Weybright and Talley, 1973.

Brooks, John. *Once in Golconda*. New York: Norton, 1969.

Chernow, Ron. *The House of Morgan: An American Banking Dynasty and the Rise of Modern Finance*. New York: Simon & Schuster, 1990.

Colbert, David. *Eyewitness to Wall Street: 400 Years to Dreamers, Schemers, Busts and Booms*. New York: Broadway Books, 2001.

Davies, Howard, and David Green. *Global Financial Regulation: The Essential Guide*. Polity Press, 2008.

Eichengreen, Barry. *Global Capital: A History of the International Monetary System*. Princeton, NJ: Princeton University Press, 1996.

Engel, Louis, and Peter Wyckoff. *How to Buy Stocks*. New York: Bantam Books, 1976.

Enriques, Lucas, and Matteo Gatti. "Is There a Uniform EU Securities Law after the Financial Services Action Plan?" Available at SSRN: http://Ssrn.Com/Abstract=982282

European Central Bank. "The Developing EU Legal Framework for Clearing and Settlement of Financial Instruments." Legal Working Paper Series, No.1/February 2006. Klaus M. Lober, 2006.

European Central Bank. "Payment and Securities Settlement Systems in the European Union." Blue Book, 4th ed. European Central Bank, 2007.

Ferran, Eilis. *Building an EU Securities Market*. Cambridge, UK: Cambridge University Press, 2005.

Fifoot, C.H.S., *Lord Mansfield*. London: Oxford University Press, 1936.

Frieden, Jeffry A. *Global Capitalism: Its Fall and Rise in the Twentieth Century*. New York: Norton, 2007.

The Giovannini Group. *Cross Border Clearing and Settlement Arrangements in the European Union*. Brussels, November 2001.

The Giovannini Group. *Second Report on EU Clearing and Settlement Arrangements*. Brussels, April 2003.

Glasson, John, and Geraint Thomas. *The International Trust*. Bristol: Jordan Publishing, 2002.

Gleeson, Janet. *Millionaire: The Philanderer, Gambler and Duelist Who Invented Modern Finance*. New York: Simon & Schuster, 1999.

Grant, Kenneth L. *Trading Risk: Enhanced Profitability Through Risk Control*. Hoboken, NJ: John Wiley & Sons, 2004.

Gray, Alexander. *The Development of Economic Doctrine: An Introductory Survey*. London: Longmans, Green, 1931.

Harvey, Robert. *Cochrane: The Life and Exploits of a Fighting Captain*. New York: Carroll & Graf Publishers, 2000.

Hopper, Kenneth, and William Hopper. *The Puritan Gift*. London: I.B. Tauris, 2007.

Hughes, Jane Elizabeth, and Scott B. Mcdonald. *Carnival on Wall Street Global Financial Markets in the 1990s*. Hoboken, NJ: John Wiley & Sons, 2004.

International Organization of Securities Commissions & Committee on Payment and Settlement Systems. Securities Lending Transactions: Market Development and Implications (1999).

Jamroz, Michael P. The Customer Protection Rule, 57 Bus. Law. 1069 (May 2002).

Johnson Jr., Charles J., and Joseph Mclaughlin. *Corporate Finance*. New York: Aspen Publishers, 2004.

Jorion, Philippe. *Value at Risk: The New Benchmark for Managing Financial Risk*, 3rd ed. New York: McGraw-Hill, 2006.

Klapper, Leora, Victor Sulla, and Dimitri Vittas. "The Development of Mutual Funds around the World." *Amsterdam Elsevier Emerging Markets Review, 2004* vol 5(1).

Kolb, Robert, and James Overdahl. *Futures, Options & Swaps*, 5th ed. Hoboken, NJ: John Wiley & Sons, 2007.

Lefevre, Edwin. *Reminiscences of a Stock Operator*. New York: John Wiley & Sons, 1994.

Lindert, Peter, and Thomas Pugel. *International Economics*, 11th ed. New York: McGraw-Hill, 1999.

Lofchie, Steven. *Lofchie's Guide to Broker Dealer Regulation* Fairfield, NJ: Compliance International, 2000.

Loss, Louis, and Joel Seligman. *Fundamentals of Securities Regulation*, 5th ed. New York: Aspen Publishers, 2003.

Loss, Louis. *Commentary on the Uniform Securities Act*. Boston: Little Brown, 1976.

Lowenstein, Roger. *When Genius Failed: The Rise and Fall of Long Term Capital Management*. New York: Random House, 2001.

Manning, Bayless. *A Concise Textbook on Legal Capital*, 2nd ed. Mineola, NY: Foundation Press, 1981.

McCormick, Roger. *Legal Risk in the Financial Markets*. London: Oxford University Press, 2006.

McIntyre, Hal. *How the U.S. Securities Industry Works*, 3rd ed. New York: Summit Group, 2007.

Norman, Peter. *Plumbers and Visionaries, Securities Settlement and Europe's Financial Market*. Hoboken, NJ: John Wiley & Sons, 2007.

Reynolds, Barnabas. *International Financial Markets Guide*. London: Lexis Nexis Butterworths, 2003.

Rosen, Joseph. *The Handbook of Electronic Trading*. Short Hills, NJ: Capital Markets Media, 2008.

Simmons, Michael. *Securities Operations: A Guide to Trade Position Management*. Hoboken, NJ: John Wiley & Sons, 2002.

Taleb, Nassim Nicholas. *The Black Swan: The Impact of the Highly Improbable*. New York: Random House, 2007.

Teweles, Richard J., and Edward S. Bradley. *The Stock Market*. New York: John Wiley & Sons, 1998.

Torosian, Martin. *Securities Transfer: Principles and Procedures*. New York: New York Institute of Finance, 1988.

Weiss, David M. *After the Trade Is Made: Processing Securities Transactions*. New York: Penguin Books, 2006.

Wood, Philip R. *Regulation of International Finance*. London: Sweet & Maxwell, 2007.

Wood, Philip R. *Set Off and Netting, Derivatives, Clearing Systems*. London: Sweet & Maxwell, 2007.

Wood, Philip R. *The Law and Practice of International Finance*. London: Sweet & Maxwell, 2008.

Yates, Madeleine, and Gerald Montagu. *The Law of Global Custody: Legal Risk Management in Securities Investment and Collateral*. West Sussex: Tottel, 2009.

George W. Arnett, III is Executive Vice President and General Counsel of HedgeMark International LLC, an affiliate of Pershing LLC. HedgeMark is a provider of risk analytics and a separately managed account platform for hedge fund investors. Prior to joining HedgeMark, Mr. Arnett was a Managing Director and Senior Managing Counsel for Pershing, a BNY Mellon Company, where he was responsible for legal oversight for international trading and operations, securities lending, domestic trading, Pershing Prime Services, Global Securities Services, Pershing Securities Limited (UK) and Pershing Managed Account Solutions. At Pershing, Mr. Arnett chaired its International Risk Committee, was a member of its Credit Committee and Pershing Ltd.'s Risk Committee, and served on BNY Mellon's Emerging Markets Portfolio Management Committee.

Index